Stepping
Showbusiness

An Autobiography of an ex-Windmill Girl

Simone Lloyd-Davies

The Wolfian Press

www.wolfianpress.com

Published by the Wolfian Press

ISBN 978- 1977833150

Stepping Out Into Showbusiness

An Autobiography of an ex-Windmill Girl

Contents

Acknowledgments

I would like to thank all the people who have contributed to the publication of this book, Friends and Family who have loved, helped and supported me over the years.

I am especially grateful to John Ready who motivated and inspired me to tell my story and helped in creating the narrative of the book.

CHAPTER ONE

My Family

Dance, Dance, Dance. I was always dreaming of being on the stage during my teenage years growing up in Southall. I was born on the Eighteenth of May 1922. I`m therefore Taurean, although only by a few days, but my "bull in a china shop" characteristics took quite a bit of polishing out in later years. My father could trace his lineage back through quite a long time as I recall, and his ancestry lay in French Huguenot stock. Even in the twenties there was quite a little community of Huguenots in London, enough it seems to keep a fairly well-attended and reasonably prosperous church on the go. My proud parents carried me there for my christening and I emerged to the world as Joan Grew. I was given another middle name at the time, but I detested it and allowed it to wither away just as soon as I could. I changed my name altogether some years later.

I joined a sort of ready-made family consisting of Fred and Nellie, my Father`s children by his first marriage. When I came on the scene, Fred would have been about eleven or so and a different generation and at an age when boys considered girls to be the lowest life form possible. In fact, Fred and I were never close at all. Things were totally different as far as Nellie and I were concerned. We became very best friends and true sisters until her untimely death when I was in my mid-teens.

Mother had also been married before and had certainly seen her share of the seamy side of life. Her first husband was a violent alcoholic, taking his anger out as so often happens on the nearest target, - my mother and her three children. One night he stabbed her in the back and she needed hospital treatment. She suffered a mental breakdown and remained in hospital for a long time. Her children were taken charge of by her in-laws, and they refused to give Mother any information about them.

After her recovery, she answered an advertisement in the paper for a housekeeper to a lonely widower with two young children. Dad lived in Manor Park at the time, and eventually they got married and I was born when Dad was 39 and Mother was 40. My brother Norman came along about 4 years later.

I started school at four and took to it like a duck to water. By the age of five, I was reading fluently and read everything that came my way. Although the old buildings which housed the school were far from inspiring, the things I learned within those walls and the wonderful friendships that were forged there, all worked together to make the old cliché true. They really were the happiest days of my life.

When I was six we had a very serious fire, from which Norman and I escaped by the skin of our teeth. Dad was at work and Fred and Nellie were at school. I should also have been at school of course, and I can`t remember how I happened to be at home at the time. Obviously a disastrous fire like that affected our home very badly, and although we repaired and cleaned up as best possible we never really felt safe there any more. Nothing for it then but to pack our bags and move. This time we ended up in Southall, which in those days was quite a bit outside "London Proper." Father bought the lease of another small jewellery shop in Ealing, just opposite the District Line Underground Station. We settled down to a reasonably cosy family life there in a small and rather anonymous terraced house. We were especially lucky in having a reasonably-sized garden, where I spent many happy childhood hours.

We weren`t a specially religious or church-conscious family, so there was no pressure put on me to attend a place of worship. We had a large and very popular chapel quite close to home and they had a number of quite good social events on offer. One of the high spots was the Maytime Festival, which was a sort of pageant featuring many of the chapel`s younger members. It had become known that I was some sort of part-qualified dancer, so I was asked to try my hand at a bit of choreography for some items in the festival. Naturally, I grabbed the opportunity. Who knew where it might lead? Although I did what many people thought was a good job and the dancing was generally well-received and appreciated, some of the chapel elders thought that my efforts had produced something which was rather too balletic in form. What they wanted was more like country dancing, far more in keeping with the chapel`s image and less sinful than other forms of dance. This is the type of attitude more common in those days which regarded ballroom dancing as fornication accompanied by unbearable music and ballet as not much better. Polite God-Fearing folk didn`t display their legs! Still these were the men with the power, so I never tried any similar offerings again. Not for them at any rate! A far cry from these days of the popular T. V. show Strictly Come Dancing.

It was about this time I started taking an interest in the opposite sex. I was lucky enough to have an escort almost all the time. It was all very friendly and platonic. A dead bore when viewed from today`s standpoint, I suppose. But I think it`s fair to say that far fewer of us ended up with nervous breakdowns or as single parents, so perhaps there was something to be said for innocence after all. We used to go off cycling, in pairs or parties, or rambling through the woods and fields which are now covered with houses or factories. You could get into the countryside around London far more quickly and easily in those pre-war days, but perhaps we only appreciate the advantages with hindsight. It`s just the same when you consider the weather patterns. When I look back, it seems that every single summer glowed with non-stop sunshine. We all know that it wasn`t true, but memory does tend to play some funny tricks. One of my boyfriends was a bit of a swell called Dennis, who actually had a car! She was an ancient and venerable Austin Seven, and was well past her sell-by date by the time Dennis and I had met. The old girl rejoiced in the name of "Poppet." I`m afraid she did a lot more popping than petting. She was incapable of ascending even the very gentle hills in the Home Counties, and many was the time when I had to walk uphill by her side, whilst she made puffing and grinding progress, usually in reverse gear. Her tendency to break down frequently and unexpectedly only served to make her more dear to both of us, because the pace of life was more gentle. There always seemed to be time to stop, take a deep breath and relax. In any case, most cars lent themselves to being repaired quite easily by the average clued-up motorist, even if his use of expletives was more colourful than polite.

In spite of the dead hand of The Depression, or maybe because of it, these years of the late thirties were also the heyday of the cinema, with the British Film Industry trying its utmost to emulate Hollywood, without either the cash or the weather to enable it to do anything really blockbusting. Quite apart from the major studios around London, which were almost as well guarded as the Crown Jewels and staffed by professionals, the mere proximity of the "big city" was itself quite enough to attract an army of enthusiasts of all kinds. These people swarmed all over farms, houses, barns and outbuildings, often without permission, and turned them into makeshift studios, sets and cinemas. These film makers were in the main, total amateurs and the quality of the product frequently made this all too clear. The name of the game, was however, escapism and the audiences for these rustic epics were totally unsophisticated. They tended generally to accept the marvels of the silver screen without critical comment. In any case they often had the additional thrill of seeing themselves in the finished film as unpaid extras.

One such film outfit operated on a reasonably regular basis not too far from my home, and gangs of us local girls hung around for hours when they were shooting at weekends and during the long summer evenings, in the hope of landing a bit-part as an extra or perhaps something a bit more meaty. The bright lights were still beckoning and I felt quite secure in my abilities as an artiste and who knew where, even a minor part in an amateur film could lead? As it turned out of course, the answer was precisely nowhere at all.

Whilst all these momentous and important events were going on, plans for my future suffered a minor setback. It was called World War Two. Even more significantly World War Two and a Half was being waged with great ferocity between my brother Norman and myself at home. He was fifteen and beginning to assert himself, whilst I was nineteen and considered I knew better. I was on the threshold of womanhood, (twenty one in those days), while he was just a schoolboy and there to be put in his place by me. He didn`t quite agree with this and we quarrelled bitterly and unceasingly through just about every waking hour until Mother became quite ill with the strain.

Apart from the "big sister knows best" scenario, which he was bound to resent anyway, the other main trigger for our rows was that Norman flatly refused to touch the margarine, and insisted on cornering the meagre butter ration for himself. If you looked at this objectively you couldn`t really blame him. Wartime margarine, looked and tasted more like candlewax than the nutritious foodstuff it was supposed to be. However, I was very close to the action. I considered he was being just a touch unfair and I didn`t like the stuff either, so I made no bones about saying so. Unfortunately for me, Norman was a bit of a "Mummy`s boy," and Mother did tend to side with him. To be fair, I was still "Daddy`s girl," even at the advanced age of nineteen, but he was out at work all the time, so I had no backing when I needed it.

Coupled with these domestic spits and spats, World War Two had started. Hitler and Goering`s merry men were busily re-arranging the map of London. Night after night we were forced to spend time in that most luxurious of apartments - The Anderson Shelter, which was a short tunnel made out of corrugated iron half buried in the garden with a mound of earth thrown over the top of it. In spite of its apparent flimsiness, it was a useful method of avoiding some of the bombing, and there were many cases on record where folk had only survived because they`d been in the shelter. The worst part of it was that, being half underground a lot of water tended to collect on the floor, and there was no really effective method of stopping it, collecting it, or of removing it once it was there. We shared this shelter with a neighbour and her son Philip. He and I used to hold hands as we sat close together on the wooden slat which served as a seat, obviously in total darkness. It was quite romantic I suppose, because we were still only in our teens. It made us forget the bombing going on all around us. Southall, where we lived was considered a "bomb alley", which is what we called the most frequently hit target areas, and I lost quite a few of my school and college pals during this unpleasant and very dangerous period. The dishy son became a bomber pilot luckily coming through the war unscathed. Thank Goodness!!

In spite of Philip`s romantic help I became quite fed up with wet feet night after night. I was also determined to get hold of my fair share of the butter, so I decided that there was no point in being a shrinking violet. My prowess on the sports field had motivated me to stand on my own two feet. Enough was enough, I was going to make my own way in the world. Off I trotted to the nearest recruiting office. The setup at that time in terms of growing up, might be a bit odd by today`s standards. During the War you could join the forces or be hanged for murder on reaching the age of eighteen, but you had to have written parental permission to get married and you couldn`t vote until you were twenty-one. It seems a bit crazy now, but we accepted it quite happily at the time.

CHAPTER TWO

For King and Country

My initial plan was to join the WRNS, not because of any salt water in my veins, although one of Dad`s ancestors had been a sea captain of some distinction, but mainly because I thought the dark blue uniform worn on ceremonial occasions with a white hat was rather smart. They had no vacancies for me at the time however, so I accepted a post in the women`s branch of the army called the ATS. It`s perhaps a bit odd that the female branches of the Navy (Women's Royal Naval Service) and the Air Force (Women`s Auxiliary Air Force) acknowledge that they were intended to be staffed by women. The army called us the Auxiliary Territorial Service, which could have been for anybody. Anyway, this was all they had to offer, so I signed up there and then. All the paperwork, the medical and other formalities went like clockwork and in a surprisingly short time after about only three weeks in total, I got my calling up papers. Then came a few tears when I said goodbye to my current boyfriend, who was a charming half Indian lad called Fin. A few days later I found myself in a sardine tin carefully disguised as a railway train making agonisingly slow progress towards a training camp on the outskirts of Edinburgh. I`m quite sure that somewhere along the way we must have passed another train full of Scots lads and lasses on their way to a training camp near London. Such are the marvels of military thinking as I found out later. For the moment however, I was more concerned with my own comfort, and eventually another girl and I managed to get a hoist up onto the luggage racks where we were actually able to doze off and sleep through a part of the journey.

This step into an unknown world brought tremendous benefits in many ways. In spite of the drab and uninspiring surroundings, I settled in straight away, finding myself in a barrack full of instant friends. We were all in the same boat and although we had many different reasons for joining, we considered that we were going to "do our bit for the war effort" and this was best achieved if we got on well and pulled together. Training was far more interesting and fulfilling than I had expected, covering a wide variety of activities. My only really bad experience came during an exercise in which we had a simulated gas attack. We were properly kitted out with good quality gas masks, so there should have been no problem. I panicked for some obscure reason, and actually flaked out on the floor of the gas training chamber.

On a much more pleasant note, we quickly found out that stories of traditional Scots meanness were just that. Myths and legends. As soon as they got to know us, (an amazingly quick process,) they took us into their hearts and really couldn`t do enough for us. We rarely had to pay for anything especially if we were in uniform, and crowds of well-wishers always gathered to cheer us as we marched through the streets to a fife and drum band. Most of us were still quite young, and this attention made us feel very grand and important. We were there to do a vital job and we were jolly well going to do it. I pity any German who would have crossed our path in those early days, we`d have eaten him for breakfast!

I don`t know whether my own step into uniform had anything to do with it, but Dad joined up into the Home Guard shortly after my own move into Service life. He had been a squaddie in the 20th London Regiment during the Great War so he wasn`t unused to military life. He became a very keen member of the Home Guard in fact, spending quite a fair amount of his leisure time in uniform. I`m sure he would have become an officer if he`d wanted to, but perhaps he didn`t fancy the responsibility.

The days flew past and we completed our training and prepared to leave the Edinburgh camp. My own posting was for Parson`s Barracks at Aldershot, which involved another interminable and boring set of train journeys. Passenger trains were always crowded and slow, and frequently had to stop and even be shunted aside to allow vital freight and ammunition trains to make their way past.

My first impression on arriving at Aldershot was how drab and depressing the place looked with long lines of colourless and nondescript huts stretching away into the distance. However, there was a world of difference to be found as soon as you actually set foot inside those huts. Again, the mood was of instant companionship. Let`s get down to the job girls! We didn`t really need anybody to motivate us. The world was ours!

Among my special pals was a truly lovely girl named Marjery. Unfortunately she was for a long time the butt of barrack room humour and only because she had what the other girls considered a "posh voice." She used to say things like "gel" and "orf." There`s often cruelty mixed with humour, not only in places like Aldershot. Although Marjery put on a brave face and made light of the teasing I`m sure she found it a bit upsetting. I did my best to smooth things over, and eventually the mickey-taking died a natural death. It was only then that the girls generally found out what a really smashing person Marjery was. She`d gladly do anything in her power to help anybody, asking for no reward, but being content with the benefit which her deed had brought. After some time, she was put up for OCTU (Officer`s Training), which she accepted as the golden opportunity it was. By this time of course, she`d become a really close friend to just about everybody in our block and quite a few tears were shed when she finally left us. I hope she succeeded as an officer. She certainly deserved to.

Another of the girls who was never short of friends had been "on the game" before joining up. She proved the truth of the old cliché about the "tart with a heart of gold," because nothing was too much trouble for her. Our barrack room ex-hustler went out of her way to help and do favours for the other girls and just like Marjery, did everything without thought of payment or reward. She fitted in beautifully with everybody and it was lovely not to have any form of bitchiness or smart remarks about her past life. Of course her personal situation could have provided a perfect excuse for the `holier than thou` brigade, who seem to have members just about everywhere. Perhaps those among us who would have tried it on could see they`d get nowhere anyway, or maybe we were lucky not to have anyone like that in our barrack. Who knows? Anyway, our terrific spirit of camaraderie was far stronger than pettiness and it gave us all a lovely feeling of cosiness and comfort in each other's company.

Among the outside influences who impinged on our little world was our platoon sergeant. A physically powerful mannish and "butch" character who would have made an excellent wrestler. Like most of her male counterparts, she missed no opportunity of making her presence felt. Her sister, however, who was in the same unit, was completely opposite in every way. A smart ultra-feminine girl who would have thought at least twice before saying boo to a goose. The sister Josephine had a rather unusual party piece. She used to tuck her skirt into her pants and dance on her hands. Constant practice and lots of encouragement from us made her into quite a polished performer, and a valued member of the garrison concert party to the extent that a lot of folk thought she was more elegant on her hands than right way up.

Every Wednesday we were confined to barracks for a "Bull" session. Where we carried out innumerable chores which were often unnecessary. I suppose the powers that be thought this was good for our self-discipline. The operation certainly did nothing to make the place more inviting looking, but we carried on with as much good grace as possible. One Wednesday I was busily scrubbing and polishing away at the barrack windows when "Sarge" crept up behind me, whisked me onto her shoulders and despite my full volume screams dunked me into a bath full of icy cold water. She never explained her motive for this action and I was afraid to ask in case she repeated the operation, so I`ve filed the experience away under life`s little mysteries.

In the centre of our Nissen hut was a long stretch of linoleum which had to be polished until you could see your reflection in it. This had to be done every week on Barrack Night every Wednesday. Our novel way of polishing was for us to group in sets of threes. The girl in the middle was equipped with a large rag covering her bum and tied in the front to prevent slipping. She then sat at one end of the lino, while two girls either side grabbed her legs pulling her along with as much speed as they could muster. It helped to make Barrack Night fun rather than a chore.

I had several tries to exercise my special preference for jobs hoping to secure a post as either a dispatch rider or a driver. Every time however, my application was dismissed as the posts were "fully established." Somewhere along the way, some kind person must have looked at my records and seen the terrible words Shorthand and Typing. The end result was that I was placed in a nice office behind a lovely desk and allowed to contribute to the War Effort by moving mountains of forms across tables and into various baskets. Of course I wasn`t alone. Typists with or without shorthand were ten a penny. It was all dreadfully boring and it was only the fun and companionship we found during our leisure hours that made it all bearable and worthwhile.

I`m sure many ex-service personnel will be amazed at my lyrical description of the Aldershot which they themselves came to know and loathe. All I can say is that I am describing my own personal experience and speaking as I found. To me, and it seemed to the vast majority of my ATS pals at the time, Aldershot at off duty times was a great place to be. It was full of interest and we enjoyed the sort of friendship which you can only really get in the Services.

Simone in her ATS uniform, 1941-45

At long last perhaps somebody up there took pity on me and decided I`d had enough paper shuffling. The chance came to apply for the post of Physical Training Instructor. I was so glad that I`d taken the trouble to keep myself fit and in good shape over the years. I passed the initial interview with flying colours largely because of my school athletic record I suppose.

During my teenage years I`d had a major interest in athletics, for which I seemed particularly well-suited, being naturally slim, with no need to diet or watch my weight. I enjoyed exercise in the form of dance, and because we didn`t have a car and public transport was expensive even then, we normally walked or cycled a great deal. My prowess as an athlete had progressed steadily and I had accumulated quite a few cups and medals. As can be imagined, the growth of this collection served to motivate me even further and my self-confidence had gone from strength to strength. I`d begun to find my feet, and look the world squarely in the eye. Competition and the ethos of winning against the odds became the dominant force in my little personal world, and I would not let anything get in my way. It could well have been in hindsight that I was too competitive for my own good, and it might have been advisable for me to have allowed or encouraged my character to build in parallel with my physical success. It`s a pity isn`t it, that we don`t see these things at the time?

I was carpeted by the Headmistress who told me off in no uncertain terms, for unladylike and unsporting behaviour, following a sports meeting in which I had won everything in sight. In order for me to qualify for one of the team events, it would have been necessary for me to withdraw from one of the individual races. I was totally unwilling to do this and I felt my decision was justified by the fact that I really had swept the board on that particular day. The Head pointed out to me in no uncertain terms that my selfishness in insisting on staying in all the races had robbed one of my schoolfellows of her own chance to shine. This rebuke acted a bit like a cold shower. I accepted her criticism, agreed that it was fully justified and made up my mind never to repeat such a mistake again.

Another levelling down experience came when I was selected to run for the County of Middlesex, in the teeth of strong competition from all parts of the Home Counties. As it so often does, pride went before a fall. The standard was far, far higher than anything I had been accustomed to in our local events and I failed rather dismally. Nobody wants to know the names of the runners-up. I mentally docketed this lesson, just like the Head`s telling off and appreciated its value. I was young and resilient however, and soon bounced back.

During my interview for the post of Physical Training Instructor at Aldershot I worked really hard to project a professional sort of image and achieve a good result. When confirmation of acceptance for posting came through I shed many tears at the thought of no more paper and threw myself enthusiastically into this new venture. The Army sent me on a total of three courses, each dealing with different aspects of exercise and programmed fitness. I thoroughly enjoyed each one and my hard work was rewarded with passes with distinction in each of the courses. This was even better than I had ever hoped for. I ended up with one of the four highest awards in the entire U.K. There was a tremendous fuss made about this at the time I remember and along with the other three highest markers, I was presented to the very top brass of the ATS at a special ceremony.

When I came back down to earth and Aldershot, I found that there had been an influx of Canadian troops to the camp. They were altogether different from the Yanks. We`d all heard tales about "overpaid, oversexed and over here." So we were just a tiny bit wary, keeping men with Transatlantic accents carefully at arm's length. We soon found that there was a definite difference as soon as you got over the Canadian border. The maple leaf lads could fairly be described as superior in virtually every way. It wasn`t long before liaisons developed and I was no exception, becoming heavily attracted to one of their sergeants. The feeling was mutual it appeared and we swiftly progressed to being quite a bit more than just friends. When he got around to proposing, I was happy to accept. In those days, even becoming engaged didn`t mean that you handed over the key to bedroom door or chastity belt. As it turned out I was to be rather lucky in that respect.

I floated around hopelessly in love and on cloud nine for quite a little while I suppose until a summons from our corps commander brought me crashing back to reality. My sergeant`s C.O. had somehow found out about our little affair and told my boss that my ever-loving beau was in fact a very much married man with four children. Our officer lost no time in putting me wise, thereby maybe, saving me from the well-known fate worse than death. Somebody up there was still looking after me it seems.

Alarms and excursions came and went, most of them pretty mild and uninteresting by today`s standards, but at least they served to break up any feeling of monotony we might have developed. One of the more exciting events happened when we found out about a Peeping Tom who was seen apparently looking through the window of one of the huts in the girls section of the camp. We were all prepared for the night, complete in many cases with curlers and face cream and most of us were wearing our Army issue striped pyjamas, generously cut in fashionable winceyette. God alone knows what sort of a thrill this would have been for anybody, but perhaps the bloke had been dared to peep in at us, or the whole thing was the subject of a bet. Anyway, we were young and pretty fit and active, and generally had a "what the hell" attitude to life not to mention that we were b****y annoyed.

We decided to give the guy a good run for his money. So a gang of us piled out of the hut with me the PTI fairly well in the lead. We`d covered quite a fair bit of ground when I suddenly felt, rather than heard a whizzzz past my ear, closely followed by another one. It took just a couple of microseconds for me to realise that somebody had alerted the sentry who was firing his rifle in the general direction taken by the intruder. Nobody it seems had warned him (or perhaps he didn`t care), that quite a few of his own side might be out there as well. Another case of somebody up there looking after me? With flying bullets as an incentive we gave up the chase and very carefully made our way back to our hut. We were greeted there by our C.O. and treated to a fine dressing down for putting ourselves at risk. We did wonder what her attitude and reaction would have been if the fellow had been looking through her own bedroom window. There was no repeat of the incident. Perhaps the bloke hadn`t realised that bullets could become involved. I`ve wondered since just what would have happened if we girls had actually caught him. Perhaps the unkindest cut of all? One thing is certain with a gang of us and in the dark, he certainly wouldn`t have got away scot free. So perhaps it`s just as well things turned out as they did.

I`d proved my worth in the tests to become a PTI, and I was as keen as mustard to get the other girls involved in my fitness training programme. I also cherished quite a strong hope of some promotion, because my opposite numbers in the male part of the Army were automatically made up to sergeant, as this gave them a bit of clout when dealing with reluctant exercisers. Unfortunately for me and many like me, the sex discrimination regulations were still some fifty years off, so the members of the ATS hierarchy were easily able to wriggle out of things by using the remarkably erudite phrase that there was "no establishment." In all my time in the service I never found anyone who could properly explain just what this phrase was supposed to mean. The effect was perfectly clear however, and I remained a buck private for some time. Perhaps somebody spotted my low morale at some time, because I was eventually offered a single, solitary stripe. WOW! Think of it. Little me as a complete, large as life lance-corporal! I forget exactly how much more I was going to be paid after promotion, but it certainly didn`t run to a bottle of champers to celebrate.

Even this trip to the dizzy heights didn`t last long, I was forever on some sort of minor charge or other. Although I really enjoyed my time in the ATS the finer points of military discipline didn`t sit comfortably on my shoulders and I suppose I was the last one to be issuing orders about King`s Regulations to my fellow squaddies. My sins included such things as being late back after a night out and wearing non-issue togs like khaki silk stockings instead of wearing the lisle cheapo ones I should have had, or something REALLY serious like wearing an officer`s tie. I also regularly wore my PTI`s crossed swords badge, because I was very proud that I had earned it, and because of all the damned hard work I`d put in. King`s Regulations dictated however, that just as with the business of promotion to sergeant, only male PTIs were actually allowed to wear the thing. Fantastic ain`t it?

In spite of all these horrendous crimes our junior commander regularly turned a blind eye and when I was sentenced to "jankers" at all, it usually turned out to be a bit of light gardening around the orderly room. Perhaps someone had told her that I was actually a bit of a keen gardener. The really grim ablutions, cleaning jobs, were awarded elsewhere. Obviously I didn`t make any sort of a fuss about this division of labour! In the end I dropped the last straw on that particular camel`s back and she sentenced me to be reduced to the ranks once again. A mock demotion ceremony was set up in the Orderly Office, at which one of the Canadian officers ripped off my stripes, whilst I stood in humility with head bowed and shaking with suppressed laughter. My barrack room mates welcomed me back as a fellow ranker once again.

The question of rank and status didn`t really worry me at all, even when I found out later on about a cousin of mine who held a commission and was a subaltern in the ATS. She lived in Guernsey until the outbreak of war at which point she came over to the U.K. and signed up. Our paths never crossed during the war, and she wasn`t really senior enough to have been able to pull any strings for me even if I`d wanted her to do so. I had only visited that part of the family on a couple of occasions before the war. Their house was a bit of a museum in some respects, because one of our common ancestors had been a sea captain, who`d brought back all sorts of nineteenth century and antique treasures from all over the world. This was the rich side of Dad`s family, but none of it rubbed off on us.

One positive thing about the situation at Aldershot was that things were quite free and easy, at least for us girls, and there was always plenty to do including heaps of dances all over the place. The Canadians, once they had found their feet were forefront in the entertainment scene organising all sorts of functions with great enthusiasm. The lads were always most generous with their candies, and they could not understand why we looked on quite simple sweets as such a fantastic luxury. The idea of rationing was of course, quite an alien concept to them.

Although virtually all the Canadians behaved impeccably most of the time, there were bound to be exceptions. A group of us got caught up in one such situation at one of the dances one evening, when we found ourselves in the company of a gang of their lads who were, to say the least, a bit the worse for drink. The atmosphere quite quickly became charged and things could have become serious. Because these things almost always escalate quickly out of control. We used a well-known feminine ploy and sought refuge in the `Ladies`. Luckily for us there was a large and accessible window through which we were able to beat an undignified retreat back to the safety of our camp.

I met and palled up with a very nice, charming French Canadian soldier in camp. He was the quiet, studious type, quite unlike so many of his boisterous fellow countrymen, and to my mind at least, totally unsuited to the profession of arms. The Canadians were virtually all volunteers and I couldn`t understand exactly what had motivated my friend to join up. Still, he owed some sort of allegiance to France I suppose and was concerned about the fate of that country under Nazi domination. We spent a lot of time together, but perhaps amazing and unbelievable in this day and age, our relationship was purely platonic as friends, and no more. He came home with me on several occasions and got on very well with my family. Perhaps my Father`s French connection had something to do with it, but it was probably more likely the way he was able to charm my Mother. He told me several times how much he appreciated the feeling of being totally at home in our company. His name was Gilles Guy Vanasse, and I`ve often wondered over the long years exactly what became of him.

My sixteenth birthday present from my parents was a brand new bicycle. Not one of today`s light racers, but a robust machine made of heavy gauge steel tubing and weighing about a ton. I`d hung on to it and had brought it along to camp with me. Several other girls also had bikes and we used up an awful lot of our off duty time going for long rides in the lovely countryside all around Aldershot. If you weren`t fit to start with, pedalling one of those and pushing it up hills would soon get your blood circulating properly. It had been an excellent birthday present and just what I had wanted. Pat who was one of my school pals and I joined a sort of unofficial cycling club based near to home. We used to go off on quite long rides into the beautiful Buckinghamshire countryside, exploring quaint market towns with romantic names. The roads were far quieter and safer for cyclists in those days, and I`m sure that motorists then were more tolerant and prepared to give cyclists a fair amount of space. The general atmosphere and feeling was that there was a lot more time to do everything. The pace of life was far more reasonable and civilised.

As well as cycling, my duties as a PTI in Aldershot involved me in organising groups to go on cross-country runs. Our favourite route crossed a small hill which everybody knew familiarly as "The Pimple." I never bothered to find out its real name, and even if I had it would still have been known and referred to as "The Pimple," so it did for us as it was. On one of our runs across this hill, one of the girls took a very heavy and awkward fall. She twisted herself in an effort to break her impact with the ground. Her injuries looked to us to have made a real mess of her leg and she had to be stretchered back to camp, obviously in great pain and distress. I believe she was discharged from the Service because of her injury, poor kid. Still, accidents will happen and we were generally fortunate that they struck us very infrequently.

On the topic of health, I`d received a warning from my Mother who was one of the old school that I must at all times and at all costs wear a vest. Of course one of my first actions on joining the ATS where I was to be treated as a grownup was to consign this wonderful garment first to use as a polishing rag and then to the bin. When she found out about this Mother was initially a bit put out, but seeing over quite some time that I was always as fit as a flea and in peak condition, she eventually accepted that perhaps that I wouldn`t come to any great harm at all.

The only real exception to my general health and fitness hit me on my 21st birthday of all days, when I was struck down with quite a severe attack of jaundice. It was a bit too much for the camp sick bay to deal with so I was transferred to the nearby military hospital. One of the high spots of my time there came when we were due to be visited by a male officer of a stratospherically high rank. His visit to the hospital was something to do with an inspection of us patients and our kit. Nothing remotely concerned with medical matters or calculated to help cure us. We were told in no uncertain terms that all those who were well enough would stand by their beds properly at attention. The rest of us who couldn`t get up were ordered to LIE to attention! It`s a grand life in the Army. So much impression did this inspection make on us that I can`t recall even the slightest detail these days. The hospital ran as I`ve already indicated, on military lines, and the nursing staff, just like we squaddies were subject to rigid discipline. Matron`s eagle eye was everywhere and she ruled even the doctors with an iron hand. Sometimes, looking back and almost certainly because I can cover it with fifty years nostalgia, I actually wish personally that we still operated under a similar regime, with respected disciplinarians to rule today`s society.

CHAPTER THREE

Stars in Battledress

On my discharge from hospital I found out that an Army show was actively looking for additional bods to join their concert party. The man in charge was George Black, whose representative in the Aldershot area was a Sergeant Corry. He adopted the stage name of Michael Ronnie, and was quite well known in theatrical and musical circles at the time and for quite a few years afterwards. He`d actually been a member of the world famous Diaghilev Ballet no less, and had developed a sophisticated Adagio dance routine. A balletic dance with lots of lifts and spins. His partner was Prudence Gwynne, who was one of the ATS subalterns at Aldershot at the time. this included lots of lifts and spins I joined the troupe as a solo tap dancing artiste, but somebody must have liked my act because I was offered the chance to take Prudence`s place when she fell sick. Obviously I didn`t wait to be asked twice! It was the sort of opportunity of which many a Hollywood epic has been made, and of which showgirls dream. We toured all the garrison theatres throughout the whole of Southern Command, and there were quite a few of them in those days. We also appeared at the Stage Door Canteen in London. This was a top drawer show, featuring many well-known artistes of all kinds and was regularly broadcast on the Forces Network by the BBC. Michael Ronnie as you can imagine, was an extremely fine dancer and choreographer. Some of his rehearsals were executed in Army Boots still dancing with such dexterity. He was very concerned about his weight often looking at himself in the mirror saying "God, my stomach is bulging." Which it wasn`t.

We were appearing in London at the period of the war when the doodlebugs were at their height. Although christened as a sort of triviality by Cockney humour, these doodle bugs were actually quite horrific in their concept and their effects. They were self-propelled flying bombs, each one carrying a large amount of high explosive and just enough fuel precisely calculated to get them over London from their launching pads on the French coast. They flew with a characteristic pop pop pop noise, which stopped abruptly when the fuel ran out. As soon as that happened and in a truly unnerving silence the bomb would plunge to earth, destroying buildings and people over quite a wide area. We operated on the well-known `The Show Must Go On` principle. What else? And carried on regardless. We also put on a pantomime, covering a period of a couple of weeks either side of Christmas, which went down very well.

B Company, ATS, Parsons Barracks, Aldershot
Simone on the far right of the front row

Even in the thick of all this frantic activity, I remained a fully paid-up member of the fife and drum band. Luckily for me, we only ever played one tune - The Road to the Isles - which I was able to manage pretty well without too much need to practise. We played this tune all the way to accompany church parades and the like. The marching troops seemed not to care about the monotony of hearing a single tune over and over again and we band people enjoyed ourselves hugely. Someone decided however, that we should progress from fifes and start playing bugles instead. Bugles! I ask you! Apart from being about the least musical of any of the instruments you can think of, because it only produced a total of five different notes, it struck me as being a touch unfeminine. I decided enough was enough and the band and I parted company.

One of my particular friends at home in Southall was Chris who was half Dutch. We had lots of fun together because she and her mother would throw parties at regular intervals and at the slightest excuse. We played forfeits, among other games. Quite innocent ones I might add. One which I remember especially well, involved one of the lads to climb up two telegraph poles. One at a time of course, and tie a cord between them and drape toilet rolls on the cord right across the road. This bit of decoration caused quite a bit of concern to the neighbours the following morning. At this time toilet rolls were the exception rather than the rule in many households. An awful lot of folk, even quite well off families used squares of newspaper. This misuse of what was, to many people, a luxury item was almost unforgivable.

Growing up in the thirties was a world removed from today`s teen-oriented society. Even at fourteen or fifteen we girls, or at least the majority of us were still very naive and ignorant of even the basic facts of life. We were going by bus on some sort of school trip one day when I remarked to my companion, although not specially loudly, that I had a pen friend in Paris and "she`s just sent me a French Letter." Instant silence, followed by a tremendous "Hrrrmph" as throats were cleared everywhere. A little later, one of my friends treated me to one of those arm around the shoulder confidences, explaining in some detail about the London Rubber Company and its connection with birds, bees and human animals. Even after her explanation, I must confess remaining quite puzzled for some time.

CHAPTER FOUR

Losing My Dear Sister Nellie

It was at about this time that we tragically lost my half-sister Nellie. She had met and fallen deeply in love with a German chap who was an extremely nice person. In fact with the most impeccable manners. In no time at all he`d popped the question and they became engaged, despite the political rumblings of the time. This was the mid-thirties, a few years after Hitler had come to power. Nellie and her fiancé were blissfully happy and spent uncounted hours talking about wedding arrangements and so forth, and had even got as far as setting a date for the big day.

Nellie and her fiancé in happier times

About a month before the wedding Nellie fell ill with what appeared to be just a simple cold. It didn`t respond to normal treatment but she carried on as we all tend to do, until the worsening of her condition forced her to take to her bed. As she showed no improvement after some time, she was eventually admitted to hospital where they diagnosed pneumonia. Her condition worsened and it seemed as if they couldn`t do anything to help her. We found out afterwards that a blood clot had formed and lodged in her brain. As she was so ill, the hospital authorities relaxed their normally strict rules about patients' jewellery and allowed Nellie to wear her engagement ring. She kept looking at it, turning her hand to and fro, although by that time the poor girl couldn`t see it at all.

My Father and I were on our way to see her one evening, and the bus seemed to be crawling along even more slowly than usual, when I was suddenly struck by the most dreadful premonition. "Daddy, I`m afraid we`ll find poor Nellie dead when we get there." I told him, barely able to get the words out. He rounded on me quite angrily "You just mustn`t talk like that, or even think it." he said. When we got to the hospital, we found my premonition was all too tragically true. She was only twenty five and had so much to live for. I lost a wonderful dear friend that night and felt her loss keenly for a very long time afterwards. Her poor fiancé was of course totally devastated and we lost touch with him very soon after Nellie`s funeral. It`s quite possible that he went back home to Germany to try and rebuild his life. I do hope he found his way back to happiness again in spite of the political problems of his homeland. He was a super chap and deserved a far better deal from Lady Luck.

I moved into what had been Nellie`s room soon afterwards, where I had a most unusual experience. I was just dropping off to sleep one night when I became aware of a light which seemed to be shining onto the bottom of the bed. It wasn`t a street lamp or anything like that.

When I looked more closely, I thought I could make out a vague figure at the foot of the bed, surrounded by the light. I got the wind-up at this and called out to my mother. She came in, and saw the apparition as well, although she never really admitted it. With hindsight, this could only have been a sort of spirit visit from Nellie, and we were foolish, not to say ashamed, to have been frightened. At the time, it was quite unnerving and mother and I spent the night in my bed holding on to each other like grim death.

In 1943, my brother Norman had joined the RAF where he was trained as a teleprinter operator. On completion of his course he was posted to Burma, of all places. In the course of correspondence at the time, and later conversations with him after the war, I was able to gather that his experiences there were far from pleasant. In common with many of the comrades involved in that sad and ill-fated campaign, he developed some mysterious tropical illness and was sick almost the whole time he was out there. The only bright spot I suppose is that he wasn`t captured by the Japanese, but even so, he knew all about what was happening, and in many places where his section had to set up camp, the stench of rotting bodies was all too evident. During his time there, Norman and I kept in touch by letter, and I hope I was able to cheer him up a little with some of my barrack room stories and humour. Norman and a friend went for a dip in the sea on one occasion. To add to the horror of Burma as it was in those days, he saw his friend drown and was unable to help him as Norman couldn`t swim a stroke. I used to dread his letters to me as I felt so helpless. It did affect my usual happy-go-lucky way of life, especially when I was on my own and the realisation of the terrible war really did come home to me.

In the meantime I got some particularly unwelcome news from home. Mother had developed cancer and was quite ill. The last thing I wanted was to add to her distress so I warned Norman to keep quiet about his own miseries in his letters home. At the same time, rightly or wrongly, to hide the truth of her condition from him, I reasoned that both of them had quite enough on their respective plates without having to worry about each other. Perhaps I was playing God. I don`t know. If I was wrong, then I can only say that I`m sorry. All I can say is that it seemed like a very good idea at the time. Although the position of being piggy in the middle wasn`t an especially comfortable one. Eventually Norman was invalided out of the service and came home, but he was a broken man. He was a shadow of his former self and his nerves were in shreds. I think it`s fair to say that he never really recovered from his experience and returned to full health.

CHAPTER FIVE

Back To Camp

On a more pleasant note, on my return to wonderful Aldershot I joined the hockey team, which was enthusiastic rather than successful or victorious. I recall particularly one very vigorous game we played against a Canadian side. It ended up in a fantastic tangle of arms and legs, with players from both sides in a sort of giant rugby scrum right in the middle of the field. The result was marked in chaos and bruises rather than goals, but all ended well. The irony of it was I suppose, that I had not one but TWO Canadian boyfriends at the time. Talk about having a foot in the enemy camp!

Camp gossip was now hinting at great moves to come in the War effort. Frissons of excitement spread like wildfire whenever any specially tasty bit of news came along. Before long, however fact had overtaken fiction with the reality of the D-Day landings and we gladly accepted our burden of working round the clock with preparations and some items calculated to help the efforts in France. Everything we did was, of course very hush-hush and this added to the nerve tingling atmosphere. Most of us were still very young and all too conscious of the awesome responsibility we all shared. As the campaign moved from strength to strength, the camp gradually emptied, like so many others throughout the country. Aldershot railway station was permanently bursting at the seams, packed with troops on their way to Channel ports for embarkation.

In spite of all the frenzied activity, and the sobering thought that many of the lads would be going from camp on a one-way ticket. Romance blossomed for me at least and I became engaged to a chap who certainly seemed to be the man of my dreams, after careful checking proved he wasn`t another married philanderer. Once bitten, twice shy! He`d been a professional footballer before the war and was fairly famous, so to avoid any embarrassment, he`d better remain anonymous. My little world collapsed around me when shortly after D-Day he was transferred at very short notice and put into a very secret camp somewhere near Hull, where he was to receive some sort of special training prior to leaving for Europe. At that time there were terribly tight restrictions on any form of travelling around the country. Hull seemed as far away as Hell, and a lot more difficult to get into! Nevertheless, Love Will Find a Way and it did too! I was able after much persistence to wangle a precious 72 hour pass. I caught the first train available, changed several times, and eventually arrived in Hull at some unearthly hour.

Everything was closed down and in almost total darkness, just like everywhere else in those days of blackout. Just to add to my burden, I wasn`t too sure of anything about my fiancé's camp and being a sort of secret place anyway, it wasn`t signposted. Several people I asked denied all knowledge of such a camp and I began to think that my ordeal of a journey was all in vain. My uniform and a few tears which I shed for good measure finally won through and my love and I were reunited for a few precious hours.

It would be lovely to report that on his return from the War we married and lived happily ever after, but it wasn`t to be. Our engagement went the way of many thousands of similar wartime liaisons. We found that distance didn`t really lend enchantment after all, and there`s something a bit frustrating about only being together via the post box. I returned his ring, shed a few tears, allowed my heart to mend itself and carried on with my life.

The next upheaval came when I was transferred from Aldershot to Bicester. Living and accommodation conditions were very similar in this new camp. The girls were the same sort of gang, from mixed backgrounds and we were still all in the same boat together. The atmosphere and ambience of the place couldn`t have been more different from Aldershot. There just wasn`t the same friendliness or spirit of camaraderie among the ATS girls at all. We were still working around the clock, but discipline was pretty extreme and confinement to barracks was the rule rather than the exception. My morale reached rock bottom, not helped by the fact that I had to shoulder another burden of form filling and paper moving, rather than being out in the fresh air and involved with PT. Under the Bicester regime, such activities as PT were accorded very low priority. My time there seemed to drag endlessly and I must record it as one of the unhappiest and most frustrating times in my entire life. Fortunately it didn`t last too long, after all.

Like many others, my time in the Service taught me the incredibly useful art of using all sorts of artifices to better my position. Of course we didn`t use such posh words as `artifices`. We called them dodges, fiddles and wangles. A rose by any other name. A lot of manoeuvring and wangling at Bicester eventually secured me a further posting and I ended up at Manorbier, a camp on the outskirts of a tiny historic village with an interesting ruined castle on the south coast of Pembrokeshire in West Wales. At the time it housed the School of Ack Ack Artillery. Ack Ack was an Army abbreviation for Anti-Aircraft. The school taught up-to-date methods of bringing down enemy aircraft by gunfire, preferably before they`d got around to dropping their loads of bombs on our cities. Actually by this time, the major thrust of the German bombing was all over, but we`d had a nasty shock on the eve of the Battle of Britain, in finding out just how vulnerable our cities were to air attack. It was therefore sensible to keep up with developments to ensure we weren`t caught out again.

Talk about moving from Hell to Heaven! This really was paradise after Bicester. The whole atmosphere was totally different. We had much more freedom and I was back in my `proper` job as PTI. Our morning classes would usually consist of cross-country runs over the clifftops and through the fields, whilst our leisure time was spent on the lovely sandy beaches or swimming in the sea. This area was considered to be a bit too far west to be likely to be invaded, so the beaches were not mined or cordoned off with barbed wire. The whole summer of 1944 was fine and warm, and we really made the most of it in every way. The war seemed very, very far away from this idyllic corner of the world.

This very special part of the world has been known for many years as "Little England Beyond Wales," and is an agricultural area where they grow lovely Pembrokeshire potatoes and raise sheep and cattle. A long time ago it appears, quite a lot of Flemish people from Flanders settled here. They could manage English but not Welsh, so the native tongue practically died out. These Flemish people were hard-working and successful farmers, so it wasn`t long before they were adopted and absorbed into the population. Nowadays there are only some place names and unusual surnames to remind us of exactly what happened.

We, for our part found that the locals couldn`t possibly have been more friendly or offered us a warmer welcome than we received. Just as we`d found in Scotland, our uniforms provided the `open sesame` to innumerable kindnesses and perks. In the next village, only about a mile down the road was a little cottage type cafe, where we could get the most delicious egg and bacon suppers. Naturally, to quote the official line, strict rationing was in force everywhere, and you couldn`t get any foodstuffs without producing your Ration Book. We asked no questions and we were therefore told no lies. We accepted the status quo with real heartfelt gratitude.

As the camp was a school and set up especially to fulfill an important training function, a large number of officers came on various courses and some of them stayed quite a while. They varied in rank from subaltern, which was the lowest commissioned rank - 2nd Lieutenant and upwards. We had a few captains and the occasional major. In my own book, they were either nice chaps or not so nice ones. I palled up with one of the nice ones and we quite often went out in a foursome. The other couple were my ATS junior commander and a friend of his. I was the lowest rank in the illustrious company. I`d never even bothered to get my lance corporal`s stripe back as it seemed too much trouble for the extra pittance involved. Anyway, we four used to go to dinner dances at the Imperial Hotel, beautifully set above one of the terrific bays in Tenby, which was only about five miles from camp. As there was an unbridgeable gulf between officers and other ranks of both sexes. I had to wear civvies. This involved me sneaking out of camp with my clothes in a holdall and changing at the hotel before making my entrance as Belle of the Ball. Social divisions were one thing, but you could always wangle a way around them if you really tried. Most of my memories of Manorbier are so very happy. It was a wonderful place where the sun always seemed to shine.

There was only one particular sad incident which comes back to me across the years. It touched my life with tragedy and made a deep impression on me apart from the loss of poor dear Nellie. I`d had precious little experience of death. I was walking across the clifftops between Manorbier and Tenby one evening in the company of my current boyfriend, when we heard a voice calling "Help, I`m dying here, please help me." My boyfriend called out that he was going to run for assistance. "Just hang on - I won`t be long." In the meantime I decided to search as best I could, to try and find the source of the voice. In that part of the world just like in Cornwall in many respects, beauty went hand in hand with great danger. The cliffs were high and rugged and no place for inexperienced climbers or fools. I was keenly aware of the nearness of the cliff edge and the night was very dark, with no real light from the moon. Common sense dictated that I`d be a lot safer on hands and knees than trying to walk upright. So I crawled gingerly towards the spot where I thought the voice originated. At last I arrived pretty close to the cliff edge, and it would have been foolhardy to have ventured further. I called out "hang on, we`ve sent for help and it will be here soon." I kept talking to try and encourage him, but as time went past, his voice grew weaker and finally faded away altogether. It was a lifeless body that the ambulance attendants recovered from the cliff face some time later. I didn`t hang about to see this, as the whole thing was quite upsetting for me. I suppose my boyfriend and I must have attended the inquest or enquiry, but I honestly can`t recall a thing about it.

Wherever there are service personnel for that matter, there`s a concert party of some sort not too far away. Many camps made up such parties from the talented chaps and girls actually on camp. Some were brilliant, others quite good and a few were awful. It was purely down to the luck of the draw. We had quite a good troupe at Manorbier and I lost no time in signing up with them. It was wonderful and I enjoyed every moment. We put on shows at the NAAFI and in the sergeants and officers messes, making a terrific hit with the audience every time - or just about. One of our efforts attracted the attention of some talent scout or other, who happened to be in the audience. As a result I was offered the chance of an audition for a well-established show called "Stars in Battledress." I passed the audition with flying colours and thought "That`s it! I`m on my way!" I wasn`t too far wrong either. The confidence I gained from the audition and the experience of working in the troupe with artistes of a high standard, formed the first really big step towards my securing a career in showbusiness.

CHAPTER SIX

Growing Up in Southall

Growing up in Southall, I`d always dreamt of being on the stage. I`d always wanted a fairy frock like most girls. The prospect of dressing up appealed very powerfully and this wish was finally granted when I was allowed to start proper ballet lessons and was fitted with a gorgeous tutu. I used to skip and prance around the garden by the hour, playing imaginary fairy games. I built a small garden for myself, using an old mirror for a lake, with a tiny model house on its shore. I dug up worms and collected snails and slugs, serving these delicacies to my dolls, who sat around us as if at a party. My other animal friend in the garden was a trapdoor spider. I used to catch flies and bluebottles on the windows of the house and feed them to my spider, placing them on her web and shaking it with a blade of grass to attract my pet to her meal.

My musical life also started at about this time and I began to study both violin and piano. It wasn`t long before I realised that I`d never get anywhere as a string player, and gave up on the fiddle to concentrate on my piano studies. I`m certain this decision was greeted with much relief by my family and neighbours because there`s surely no noise on Earth to compare with a badly played violin. To be fair though, nobody ever actually complained, at least not within my own earshot. My pianistic studies progressed steadily, but not remarkably. I was no prodigy but I did enjoy being able to make music for myself. There was never any pressure brought on me by anyone. I was allowed to be my own pace setter and I`m quite sure that this helped me. Playing the piano was a pleasure not a chore, and not just another lesson, like at school.

My ballet classes unfortunately fell victim to the Depression in the Thirties, and had to be suspended for the duration. This was partly due to the fact that people`s disposable income fell drastically often to pitifully low levels even in the prosperous suburbs of London. My Father had taken on the lease of a small jewellery shop in Leytonstone. His stock in trade was mainly paste and alloy, nothing like the jewellers in the West End and Hatton Garden where jewellery really meant something. East End jewellers spent long hours in small shops for little reward. There were some compensations however, one of which didn`t materialise until much later on. One of Dad`s fellow "shoppies" was a butcher, appropriately enough named Johnnie Grubb! When the war came along and strict rationing was in force, Johnnie was able to keep us reasonably well supplied via the Black Market. This was strictly illegal of course, but the practice was far more commonplace than the authorities would care to admit. Dad employed a man as an assistant in his shop. His wage was guaranteed via the Appropriate Wages Council, so if anyone had to go short during a poor week, it would be Dad, not him. On many occasions he had to make up his wages out of his own pocket, and we went just that little bit shorter than usual. As if to add insult to injury, Dad was waylaid on his way home one evening, a very rare occurrence in those days, and robbed of even that week`s meagre wage. There was no help of any sort. No Victim Support group or Criminal Injuries compensation, so we had to grit our teeth and carry on as best we could. It was some sort of comfort to realise that, unpleasant as things were for us, there were plenty of folk in a far worse situation than we were.

We couldn`t see much prospect of ease in the money situation so I resigned myself to giving up on the idea of dancing lessons for quite a few years. I found plenty of other interests to fill up the time and carried on in this way until I decided that I could afford to finance dancing lessons for myself out of my pocket money. I signed up at a small stage school not far from home and attended regularly. Although the school was small, it supplied quite a steady stream of pupils to take part in stage shows, and some of these were quite important "top drawer" productions. Like everybody else I suppose, I lived in hope, but I was always found to be too tall, too skinny, or just unsuitable for some vague reason or another, so my chance never came along. In fact, I didn`t get to tread the boards until I was selected for a small part in one of the schools own domestic productions. Like many others before and since. I panicked, forgot my lines and ran off the stage in floods of tears. As far as I was concerned at the time, that was IT!

My life-long friend Pat, who I had known from the age of 5

I enrolled as a student at Ealing School of Art. Like many teenagers, I still had no real idea of exactly what I wanted to do with my life, so I decided for the moment at least to concentrate on the things in which I was most interested, and in which I could achieve a reasonably high standard. This sampling of some of life`s goodies would help me concentrate before I finally committed myself. Or at least, that`s what I hoped. I was rather good at Art in particular, and found it very easy to lose myself in the lessons. The teachers were also very enthusiastic and supportive and this obviously helped a great deal.

In spite of all this, I still had a lingering hankering for the world of dance. Every Wednesday a peripatetic teacher of Dance visited the school, offering lessons in the Russian technique of Ballet. She was an ethereal, almost unreal creature, very chic, beautifully turned out and looking as if she`d just arrived from Paris. She had a long chiffon scarf, which she used to totally devastating effect as a prop and we girls were fascinated by her. My friend Patty McGuigan and I were captivated by the whole idea of the magic world which "Madame" offered, and lost no time in signing up for her classes as soon as we had the chance. We just knew we had done the right thing, and adored every minute spent in the classes. One of the fringe benefits of the dance class was that pupils were served tea beforehand. The menu will raise eyebrows by today`s standards, rather than provoke mouths to water, but there was a whole world of difference between bread and butter and jam in the thirties, compared with today`s low fat spread, stodgy sliced loaves and jam containing more `E` numbers than fruit. Food before the war was produced more naturally and tasted better as a result. We knew no different at the time and took such things for granted. Apart from anything else our appetites were not jaded or spoiled by processed foods and we were fit and active. I daresay we would have tackled pretty well anything on a plate. This small perk also helped in a small but useful way to assist in ekeing out the family`s tightly stretched budget.

Apart from the dance issue, and back down to earth, our preparation for the mundane world of earning a living was more than well catered for within the context of the general college syllabus. In spite of it being regarded as a college for the more mature student, school values and discipline still held sway and the staff generally tended to be on the strict side. Our English teacher caught Patty and I in deep conversation in the middle of one of her lessons and decided to make an example of us. She told Patty to stand and speak for two minutes on the subject of trees. This was a grave mistake on the part of the teacher. With a name like Patty McGuigan she could only have been of Irish stock and she hadn`t just kissed the Blarney Stone, she`d swallowed a whole chunk of it! Eventually the teacher admitted defeat and stopped Patty in full spate. She never ever picked on either of us again.

Two of the teaching staff were male and naturally several of the girls had terrific crushes on them. Patty was head over heels in love with Mr. White, the Merchandising master, while I had totally lost my heart to "Fooky" Foulkes who tried so very hard to teach us the mysteries of Maths. "Fooky" was actually very nondescript and in fact a little bit odd looking. His attraction for me must have been the way he seemed to go out of his way to be kind and considerate, and to pay me all sorts of little compliments. I can`t really remember anything specific, but I was quite happy to bask in these obvious proofs of his affection. Strange isn`t it, how much such small trivialities can wield such an enormous influence when you are sixteen?

The Merchandising portion of our studies contained an element of what would today be called "work experience." We were placed in temporary lowest grade and naturally unpaid positions in many of the top London stores, including Harrods, Swan and Edgar, Selfridges and so on.

I don`t think any of us went to Marks and Spencer or anywhere down market like that. Among the very few benefits attached to these very mundane, boring and rather tiring jobs would be the occasional chance to model clothes. Although these would actually come from the stores` "Junior Miss" range rather than the treasury of the main fashion departments. They of course were expensive, upmarket and well outside the range of clothes we would expect to wear in the normal course of events. As may be imagined, we grabbed at each opportunity to model these clothes and loved every minute.

After final exams, we left the Ealing School of Art with the RSA (Royal Society of Arts) certificate, which showed you had certain practical skills, and was therefore a qualification respected by the business community in those days. After qualifying in Shorthand and Typing; Dress Design; Maths; Art; Merchandising and English, Patty took the plunge directly into show business, becoming a professional singer of some renown and appearing with several of the most famous bandleaders of the day including Lou Preager and I believe, Geraldo as well. A bit more prosaically I waved my hard won certificates and put my Shorthand and Typing into gear and managed to land a reasonable job in the legal department of a firm in Wembley.

As I look back down my telescope I seem to have been blessed with an enormous, if not amazing quantity of spare time in those days, judging by the amount of activities I managed to cram into my leisure hours. Not only was I studying ballet; tap dancing; elocution and singing at a school in Hanwell, but I went skating, cycled everywhere, entered talent contests. At the age of sixteen, I landed the part of the Princess in Beauty and the Beast, and actually won a prize of a solo spot in a show featuring Elizabeth Welch, who was then really in her prime and topping the bill everywhere. I was on cloud nine about this and hoped against hope that it would lead on to something really special. For some reason, the whole thing fizzled out without trace. My debut and the days when I trod the boards for a living were still quite a long way off and I was to go through quite a few lessons in the school of life in the interim.

After three and a half years in the A. T. S. and "Stars in Battledress," had ended. My mother developed cancer. Her illness was the reason I left the Forces, leaving on compassionate grounds, so that I could look after her. I travelled back home to near London from Manorbier in Pembrokeshire, where I had served as a Physical Training Instructor attached to an Ack-Ack Training Battery. I was a civilian once again. In those days over 60 years ago, there were few, if any, wonder drugs and the onset of cancer was generally a one way street ending in death. Usually, apart from quite unpleasant treatment with radium needles and the like, all they could normally do was to administer pain killers to ease the patient along his or her way. The cancer had affected one of Mother`s breasts. and she`d had an unpleasant operation leaving her with scars across her chest, down her side almost to hip level and right down the inside of her arm. Father, Mother and I therefore settled ourselves down as best we could trying to put a brave face on things, but basically just waiting for the inevitable end. To our amazement and delight Mother was actually responding to the treatment she was getting and it was not too long before the doctors considered that her cancer was checked. I think the proper expression is that it "went into remission." Mother had secured a tremendous reprieve. Although she couldn`t regard herself as completely cured, and still needed quite careful attention to diet and lifestyle, she and therefore I, could start looking forward to some sort of future and a semblance of normality which allowed me to think about my own life, career and ambition.

One of the things that happened whilst all this family drama was going on was that the war had finished. I missed out a bit on the junketings held on VE Day (Victory in Europe) but had a wonderful time celebrating Victory over Japan, VJ Day, a couple of months later. In late summer of 1945 I decided to really let my hair down, for the first time in ages and went up to town. I ended up in the Caledonian Club of all places, where, along with a huge crowd I danced nonstop to the lovely reels and jigs. I don`t think I`ve ever known such an electric, thrilling atmosphere anywhere, before or since. It really was tremendous! By the end of it all, I looked down and was almost surprised to see that my feet were still in place. I thought I`d danced them off with all the excitement and celebration. A very tired girl found her way home at some unearthly hour, but it was all worthwhile. These things only happen once in a lifetime, or at least let`s hope so! I, for one, certainly don`t want to see another war. If it does happen, I wonder whether there`ll be anybody left alive to celebrate its end.

By now, the whole family had got its collective breath back, and we`d come to terms with the reality that Mother was going to be around for a good while yet. Such mundane things as earning a living had been pushed into the background whilst I`d been at home caring for Mother but now it was time to consider exactly what I was going to do. I still had my certificates for Shorthand and Typing of course, but I`d also had a taste of life on the stage and the idea of pounding the "working girl`s piano" in some grotty office just didn`t appeal at all. Still, I had to eat, so I took on a couple of temporary jobs, just to keep the wolf from the door, and to have something to fall back on, just in case.

CHAPTER SEVEN

After The War

One of my very first priorities was to take out a subscription to The Stage, which was the showbiz people`s bible, and THE place in which to look for adverts for all sorts of theatrical and show jobs. I was keenly aware that I was going to have to compete with hundreds, or maybe even thousands of people who`d left the Services and were also seeking stage work. Still, I`d had a useful taste through my experience in the Forces concert parties and was confident I could have a go in auditions without disgracing myself. In fact, although there were quite a fair number of auditions being offered all over the place, I considered I`d be best advised to try and stay in London, or at least within easy reach of London just in case Mother took a turn for the worse. I also thought I`d try and aim a little higher than the mundane chorus girl type of role. Perhaps I was being a bit too choosy, but I preferred to think of it as showing some discernment. After all, if I didn`t place a high value on myself and my talent, how could I expect other people to do so?

After some time, during which I`d come across nothing I considered worthwhile, an advertisement appeared which made me think "This might be IT!" The prestigious Sherman Fisher group was looking for dancers for a show to tour the Home Counties. In those far-off days, the Sherman Fisher girls were almost as well known as the Tiller Girls. I wrote a letter, wondering whether perhaps I had set my sights a little high for starters, but at the same time thinking "Well, Nothing Ventured, Nothing Gained." I was delighted to receive a letter inviting me for an audition/interview. I attended the audition which was held at No.11, Great Newport Street in the West End of London.

This was an important meeting place for aspiring stars. In the rehearsal rooms on the first floor were gathered about 40 girls in rehearsal kit. At the end of the long room two figures were seated. One was a stout, pretty and genial looking lady, about thirty five years of age. The other was a short, slight man of about fifty years of age with lank, dark hair, a yellow face and teeth to match, who was the great Mr. Sherman Fisher himself. The pretty lady was his wife.

One by one the girls carried out their routines under the close scrutiny of the Sherman-Fishers. Some were quite good, but others were obviously wasting everybody`s time. I was about fifteenth in line, so I stepped forward gave it my very best shot, and then sat down with everybody else for a seemingly interminable wait whilst our pair of adjudicators went into a huddle, whispering to each other and comparing notes. Then we were sorted out into yesses and noes. He required twenty four girls as he had three shows to go out on the road. Of course, we all had to wait around to learn the results, and to be weeded out. I was one of the lucky ones, although Mr. Sherman Fisher was not too enthralled with my tap dance offering. He thought there was a lot to be desired there. But my ballet made up for the tap shortcomings, and he said that he would take me on. During my teen years I had been to Madame de Courcey`s classes for tap dancing lessons. However, ballet was my favourite, so I didn`t take very well to tap dancing. I was a square peg in a round hole and was never chosen for pantomime. I realised that a man with his background wouldn`t normally offer criticism unless it was deserved and constructive, so I took his remarks on board and determined that he would have no cause to pull me up in future.

One really special bonus of this audition was that it led to my meeting one of the most wonderful people I`ve ever known. She was called Pat, and we hit it off together immediately. We became firm lifetime friends and eventually shared digs. As a start, she took me under her wing to rehearse my tap routines over and over, until I became a quite polished and confident performer. I`ve always blessed Pat for the endless patience she showed and for her encouragement whenever I felt a bit down. After all this tap dance business could have meant make or break for my future career. As it turned out, I became so good under her tutelage that I ended up as quite a good tap dancer. Later on I was promoted to be Head Girl of the whole troupe after the original holder of the post left the show to get married.

Pat Hamilton

Obviously I couldn`t take such a large step without some backing, so my parents and I sat down around the table and discussed the whole question at some length. I reminded them that I could always put my shorthand and typing skills to use if it ever became necessary to give up my showbusiness ambitions, but at the same time I felt that such talent as I possessed deserved to be recognised and that I ought to be given the opportunity to at least try things out. My parents bless them, agreed wholeheartedly and Dad offered me a loan without strings or interest, of eighty pounds so that I could get some quality clothes and good makeup. I know that this sum will only buy a half-tidy pair of shoes these days, but in the mid-forties you could put a fairly substantial wardrobe together and still have a reasonable amount of cash left over for powder and paint for eighty quid. This gesture touched me deeply because I remember only too well the lean times of the thirties when we didn`t even have the makings of a proper meal on quite a few occasions. I accepted his generosity with gratitude, and a huge hug and a kiss, and assured him that it wouldn`t be long before I`d be earning enough to pay back what I regarded as a true debt of honour.

Simone, Eastbourne 1946, Sherman Fisher Co

The first show in which Pat and I were involved was titled "Spotlight Scandals." We had the spotlights of course, but anybody expecting to see anything scandalous must have been very disappointed. The star was a chap who went by the name of Scott Saunders, and who had composed the show`s signature tune. A number called Rolling around the World. Although this was quite catchy, it never made anything of an impact. The show too, went the way of the tune, and folded up completely after about six months. Although we were obviously very disappointed, at least the show had given us some worthwhile opportunities, and we`d worked Great Yarmouth, Brighton and Eastbourne during a particularly good summer season. Naturally we made as much as we could of the glorious weather and most of our daytime leisure hours were spent lazing on the beaches or swimming, with only occasional need for rehearsals to help iron out any little flaws in the show.

We had a couple of odd experiences with digs during the tour. At one house, the landlady`s son, who had what is today known as Down`s Syndrome took some sort of violent dislike to my coat, which I`d left hanging behind the bedroom door. He ripped it to pieces, and I`m sorry to say that his mother didn`t have the gumption to offer me any sort of compensation for it. However, we did get a sort of second-hand revenge in an odd way. The toilet arrangements at this place were archaic to say the least, and one member of our company objected most strongly to having to walk right down the garden to the loo. She used to "water" the landlady`s aspidistra plant instead. At the time, Pat and I thought that this was a disgusting way to carry on, but looking back, perhaps it was a peculiar sort of poetic justice on the landlady after all. I couldn`t blame the son for what he did - he didn`t know any better. But nevertheless, his mother`s lack of principle was really something else.

With the demise of Spotlight Scandals, Pat and I made up our minds that although the future looked a bit uncertain, we were going to stick together and put a brave face on things. Our fears of the Dole proved groundless however, and we were lucky enough to be taken on almost immediately" for "Venus Steps Out." This show starred a couple, quite well-known at the time, named Gaston and Andree, who had developed an exceptional and very sophisticated adagio dance routine. Andree herself was also responsible for the staging of a rather special and tasteful nude tableau. All very artistic and professionally presented. In those days, whilst nudes were acceptable on stage, they had to remain completely still throughout the whole routine. If they had moved at all, the show would have been declared obscene by the Lord Chamberlain`s Department and closed down. The theatre management and any responsible members of the stage company would also be hauled off to court, to be faced with quite heavy fines on conviction. The Lord Chamberlain`s office quite frequently sent officials to attend stage shows all over the country incognito, and it was their job to report any infringements of this rather batty law to their department. Why a moving woman should be any more obscene than a static one, was something I have never been able to work out. It never affected me, as I was never personally involved as a nude. Our costumes were frequently on the scanty side, but they stopped short of complete exposure.

Anyway, Andree and her girls stayed firmly within the law, and there was never a whisper of anything untoward about any of the nudes, nor of Andree`s management or presentation. She herself was an exceptionally beautiful woman. My own part in the show was as one of a trio of girls presenting a song and tap dance act. Hard work and regular rehearsals ensured that we were pretty good, so we looked forward with great optimism to a long and successful run with the show. Right from the start the show seemed dogged with the worst possible luck. At dress rehearsal the orchestra played the National Anthem. This was NEVER done at rehearsal and all we members of the cast were horrified. It was inviting disaster. Along with sailors, stage people are exceptionally superstitious, and indeed, dreadful things began to happen to the company. By far the worst, truly a great tragedy was the sudden death of our acrobatic dancer, a particularly talented youngster of only seventeen. The post mortem revealed that she was pregnant, but she`d kept this little secret hidden from us right to the end. Soon after this, several members of our Hungarian Juggling and Acrobatic Troupe suffered falls and broken limbs, ruining not only their act but a proud record of fitness and freedom from injuries throughout their history of many years on stage. The last straw came when Andree suffered a serious mishap in her dance routine with Gaston. She miscalculated during a quite dangerous and intricate lift and fell awkwardly. Although no great height was involved, she had to be rushed off to hospital where she remained out of action for a considerable time.

We played at Clacton during the summer season, right in the middle of a heatwave. Pat and I were serious and confirmed sun worshippers at that time and we grabbed at every opportunity to head for the beach. One day, I suppose it was bound to happen anyway, we stayed out far too long, fell asleep in the sun and awoke feeling terrible. We made a rather sheepish entrance to the theatre, looking like a pair of overdone lobsters. We had burned ourselves quite badly and our costumes, made largely of net and sequins tortured us right through the show. To add the final coup de grace, Gaston, our producer had steam coming from his ears when he saw the state we were in, and gave us a very severe dressing down. We couldn`t say much, as we deserved the row, and perhaps we were lucky that he didn`t sack us there and then.

Some time later, we terrible twins were involved in another incident. As if to prove that neither of us would qualify to play Little Miss Goody Two Shoes. It was during the run of the same show, but we had moved quite a bit further North by this time. Pat and I had developed quite a keen interest in dog racing of all things. Please don`t ask me why! We`d nothing in our background to explain this. We were sitting in a cafe, one day, deep in a head-to-head discussion about a quite important dog racing meeting which was to be held that day in Doncaster. Sunny Donny, which is what the racing fraternity have christened the town, wasn`t too far away, and we decided that we could get there, see at least some of the action and get back in time for that evening`s performance. A group of five men was sitting around a nearby table and had obviously been earwigging our conversation. Eventually they chipped in, telling us that they were a gang of bookies, who were actually on their way to the self-same meeting that we`d been discussing. They invited us along, assuring us that there would be no strings attached, so after a little hesitation, Pat and I decided to go along with their offer. As well as free transport and the "total enjoyment" of being in their company, they actually gave us a whole fiver to have a flutter. Five pounds was no mean sum in those days. Many men worked a whole week for less, especially in the really mundane jobs, and it was also quite a bit more than we were earning as showgirls. After another bout of conscience wrestling, we decided to accept the cash, and we ended up having a marvellous time.

We got back to the theatre in plenty of time to sort ourselves out for the evening performance, but I can`t recall how we ended up cash-wise. We couldn`t have shown much of a profit on our betting, because I`m sure I would have remembered if we had. At the end of the day, it`s almost always the bookie who wins. On the subject of bookies, we thought the whole escapade was over and done with. No such luck. A rather rude shock was on its way and it wasn`t too long in coming. At some time during our conversation with our racing companions, we must have let slip that we were working at that particular theatre. Be that as it may, we finished the show as usual, when all Hell broke loose backstage. Our bookie friends, full to the gills with booze had burst in, demolished the poor old stage door keeper and were parading all over the place looking for us. Gaston, summoned to try and sort things out, told us to make ourselves scarce. So we climbed up right into the flies - the sort of attic, high above the stage - where we stayed hoping to be "out of sight out of mind." We had a bird`s eye view of what had become a real free-for-all, with fists flying all over the place. Luckily our "friends" were so drunk that few of any of the blows actually landed, but the incident wasn`t finished until the police arrived, restored some semblance of order, and carted the belligerents away.

Then of course, there had to be a post mortem. The following morning, early but not too bright, the pair of us were on the carpet again. Gaston, who had his share of worries anyway, really ripped into us this time, and we were within a gnat`s whisker of being sacked. In all conscience there were plenty of other girls looking for jobs like ours, and it wouldn`t have been too difficult for Gaston to have replaced us almost immediately. It was only after a large slice of humble pie and promising on pain of death that nothing like this would ever happen again, that Pat and I secured our reprieves. We were fully aware of the need to be grateful, and decided that we`d be best advised to watch our steps in future.

Life in the theatre wasn`t all sunbathing and the excitement of hairsbreadth escapes. It had its downside as well. For a start not everyone was as tolerant as Gaston had proved himself to be, and we had some really rough times with other management staff and producers. Although it was interesting touring and seeing different parts of the country, we were living out of suitcases and dependent on the tender mercies of landlords and landladies to provide digs for us. Some of these were decidedly grotty to say the least, and they weren`t always the cheaper ones either. Money was always a problem week after week and once the rent was paid, there was usually a pittance left over. Out of this we had to feed and clothe ourselves. So many of our meals consisted of "POM" a sort of stone-age version of today`s "Smash" and all the other powdered potatoes. POM just didn`t taste right at all, and we had to use milk and some of our precious butter to try and make it a bit more palatable. Its sole virtue was that it was cheap. We were always hungry. Not too surprising perhaps when you consider our particularly energetic lifestyle. Dancing for hours in the bright lights is a wonderful way to burn up calories.

One Lancashire town, which had better remain anonymous for fear the good people who live there might take umbrage, provided us with what must have been the worst digs ever. The place was infested with lice, and many of them and their associated nits ended up in our hair. It`s a good job we were such close friends to start with, because this little episode meant many long and quite unpleasant sessions with fine toothed combs and frequent hair washes in medicated shampoos. These were made to be effective rather than cosmetic or sweet smelling and both Pat and I went around ponging like chemists shops for quite a while. Ironically perhaps, we were probably the fussiest pair in the whole show when it came to personal hygiene and cleanliness. Whenever possible we took a daily bath and were always most particular about having clean and fresh clothes.

Another near disaster hit us when we arrived very late at night in a strange town. When we finally located our digs, we found to our horror that they had been double-booked, and there was no room at that particular inn for us. We`d been travelling by train for hours, so we were worn out and felt filthy and dishevelled. Ah! The joys and delights of a career in showbiz!! Nothing for it but to hump our luggage and tramp around the streets to see what we could find. As I`ve indicated the town was strange to us and we were probably wandering aimlessly without much hope, or any real clue about what parts of town were likely to be most fruitful. In the end we turned up at a police station and asked for their help. They couldn`t offer us much, unless as one facetious young constable suggested we were to go and hurl a brick through somebody`s window. Joking apart, however, they soon realised that we were in a bit of a mess and detailed one officer to accompany us in our search. By now, it was very late indeed but we trudged on until, by a seeming miracle, we were offered overnight shelter in the office of a friendly cinema manager. We were completely worn out, so we accepted his kindness and promptly flaked out on the floor, totally exhausted. The next day promised us a repeat performance and we spent even more precious hours just walking around with high hopes. At last, our luck turned and we succeeded in finding what turned out to be very reasonable, comfortable digs.

As with any other aspect of life, I suppose, there were entries on the plus side as well as the minuses. One town in the South of England which again I shan`t name had one of the most wonderful eateries we`d ever come across. For the very modest sum of 1s.6d. (seven and a half pence today) we could help ourselves to as much salad as we wanted. And go back for seconds! Obviously we looked on this place as heaven on earth and went there every day for the whole time we were playing in that town. I can`t imagine there being anything like that sort of generosity still available these days, but you never know, do you?

I sometimes wonder whether today`s theatre and show people have the same problems, trials and tribulations as we had to endure. It`s rather unlikely, I suppose because there are comparatively far fewer of them about. Even in our day the music hall aspect of live theatre had started to decline although we never had much trouble in attracting an audience wherever we went. As well as these live shows cinemas were packed, there were all sorts of dances everywhere and always something to do and somewhere - quite apart from pubs and clubs - to go, usually at reasonable prices. Another bonus was that you could be fairly sure of getting home in complete safety, even through city centres. Urban areas were certainly not the jungles they have now become. Television hadn`t destroyed conversation and although we`d just come through a particularly bloody war, everyone seemed to care more than just a little bit about their fellows.

The shows in which Pat and I were appearing, weren`t just processions of scantily clad and naked girls. There was a bit of comic relief as well, and a succession of comedians came and went. Many of the audience regarded the comic as a nuisance and an interruption, and it said a lot for the lads that they frequently succeeded in turning the whole thing on its head and taking a couple of curtain calls. One of the better comics was Bernard Spear, who was already quite well known on the circuit, and had an excellent line in patter. He`d been around for years and had, it seemed, seen and done just about everything in all corners of the country. As a result of this background he had a wealth of experience to recount and we sat spellbound for hours as he reeled off story after story and dropped names right left and centre. It seemed that he had a particularly soft spot as far as Pat and I were concerned, and gave us all sorts of little tips about how to push ourselves forward. He told us, amongst other things that we had to make our own way against the odds and to expect much more criticism than praise. We in turn confided to this sort of "father figure" all our ambitions and plans. Naturally we didn`t want to spend the rest of our lives playing the small provincial theatres, although we were fully aware that this was probably the best sort of apprenticeship we could expect to get. As far as Pat and I were concerned we wanted the really bright lights, fame and extra money that could be got by playing the top London spots. Bernard told us about his own time at the Windmill, where he spent quite a lot of his initial career, and told us we had to take the bull by the horns if we were really serious about getting anywhere.

Then as now, the best jobs were rarely if ever, advertised, and you had to show initiative and jump in with both feet if you wanted to get on. Coming from a man - no I`ll pay him the justified compliment of calling him a gentleman which is what he always was to us - of Bernard`s calibre, this was pure gold, especially when he promised in total sincerity that he`d be glad to add his personal recommendation to help us on our way. This was said in a spirit of fellowship and goodwill. He meant every word and we valued it. After mulling things over, we decided that we`d be daft as well as ungrateful to pass up any opportunity to get ahead. It seemed as if Bernard`s path had crossed ours by a welcome stroke of Fate. So, for Heaven`s sake let`s get on with it! We duly put pen to paper and after many re-writings and alterations, sent off our applications together with the most flattering photos of ourselves which we could find, to the great Vivian Van Damm at the Windmill. We looked on this as akin to having written to the King himself and had very mixed feelings about whether such a great showbiz figure would put himself out to answer us.

The days went by and we`d resigned ourselves to hearing no more, when back came a letter with a London postmark. Ever tried opening an envelope with your fingers crossed? The letter inside expressed interest in our application and offered both of us an audition. We didn`t know whether to laugh or cry. A giant step had been taken and we could well be on our way at last.

So there we were off to "The Smoke" after all. We had to present ourselves and show our skills to a selection panel of three. They were the Windmill`s dance arranger Maisie Cryer; Keith Lester who was one of the top choreographers of the day and an exceptionally talented dancer in his own right; and at the top of the heap, as it were, Vivian Van Damm, the great man himself. He looked terrifying, wearing a stern expression and sporting an enormous cigar, just like Winston Churchill. We found out later that also like Churchill, he was rarely if ever to be seen without a cigar in his mouth, but we never looked closely enough to make out whether it was lit or not.

Pat went in first and I sat on broken glass for what seemed like hours until she returned and ushered me in. I needn`t have worried about Pat as it happened, because she was a most competent and polished performer, and came through her audition with flying colours. I don`t know whether my own less than perfect effort in front of the Sherman Fisher set up came back to haunt me but Pat`s own positive attitude encouraged me, as well as the realisation that if she passed and I failed, there was the end of a truly wonderful friendship. Anyway, in I sailed with a stomach packed tight with butterflies and shaking all over. I got through my routine quite well, knowing I hadn`t made any serious mistakes. By the use of that marvellous invention called hindsight, I`m quite sure that I could and should have done better, but at the time, we`re not quite so wise are we? I finished my offering thinking "Well that wasn`t TOO bad, but the decision could go either way." The three bosses went into a huddle, and eventually decided that I`d be OK. Pat and I were going to stay together after all. Sometimes life really can be great. We had to wait for some six weeks before rehearsals were due to start, but we were put on the books with immediate effect and paid a retainer of four pounds a week. This in itself was fantastic but even more wonderful was the promise of a starting wage of £8.10s.0d per week. Many people at that time especially the younger inexperienced factory girls would have counted themselves lucky to have earned that amount in a month. I learned later on that if Mr. Van Damm REALLY liked you, then the sky was the limit. I myself was never one of his "blue-eyed girls," but I was in regular, well-paid employment and able to keep the wolf from the door.

Pat and I left the audition rooms walking on cloud nine as well may be imagined. After strolling, giggling and talking for a short distance, reality suddenly reasserted itself and we realised that we were quite peckish. We were ladies of some means now and decided to indulge ourselves just a little. We turned ourselves in the direction of the Express Dairy Cafe in Great Newport Street. This cafe had established itself as a well-known and popular meeting place for theatre and stage folk and also for film artistes and we felt very strongly that this was just the sort of place to which we now belonged! We had cash to spend and keen appetites too, so in we waltzed without a second thought.

CHAPTER EIGHT

Temptation Harbour

Whilst we sat there enjoying our coffee and looking around to see if we could " talent spot," Pat leaned over and whispered that a chap at a nearby table appeared to be hypnotised or something, because he seemed unable to take his eyes off me. To be honest, I didn`t notice him for myself, because I am more than a little short-sighted and far too proud (or whatever the proper word might be) to wear my specs. Pat nudged me again and whispered that he had got up and was moving in our direction. He came over to our table and asked most politely if he could join us and talk to us for a moment. He introduced himself as William Hartnell who had starred in the first Carry On film and was the original Doctor in Doctor Who in later years. At the time he had a leading role in a film being shot in the area around Welwyn, in Hertfordshire, quite a distance North of London. The film was called "Temptation Harbour," and William`s co-stars were Robert Newton, Irene Handl, Margaret Barton and most significantly as far as I was concerned Simone Simon. William had been struck by the uncanny resemblance between me and Simone it appears. He apologised for staring at me explaining that the Director was going frantic trying to find a stand-in for Simone for a couple of scenes. He asked whether I would possibly be interested and suggested that it would be best to strike while the iron was hot and asked if I would come along with him so that he could phone the Director. I told him that of course I was interested - who wouldn`t be? - but at the same time preferred to be a bit cautious. I was naïve but not THAT naïve and said that I`d go along with him but only if Pat came with us as a chaperone. William agreed immediately assuring me that everything was completely honest and above board. Off we went as a trio.

William made his telephone call and encouraged me to speak to the Director myself. The result was an invitation to attend an interview and tests on the following day.

This was exciting stuff! Little me in a major film and that`s just for starters. On a more mundane topic, the first drawback was that I had to get myself to Welwyn Garden City by 7.00 a.m. Public Transport was much more available and flexible in those days, and although it meant getting up at the crack of dawn and losing quite a fair bit of my beauty sleep, I managed to get there on time. As soon as I arrived and introduced myself, I was whisked away to make-up, looked at carefully by Wardrobe, provided with a white satin swimsuit and shown into a dressing room with directions to change as quickly as possible and make myself comfortable to wait for the Director.

After what seemed to be a lifetime, he turned up accompanied by Simone Simon herself. They were both struck, just like William had been by the resemblance between us, and I was offered the job there and then. A short interview/audition followed after which there was a long session during which they took a tremendous number of still photographs. I hugged myself with delight at the thought that at last I`d made the big time. Star billing and name in lights had to be just around the corner, or there was no such thing as justice!

Of course, there had to be some sort of a snag. And there was! What they had conveniently omitted to mention at that first interview was that I wasn`t to be just a double for Simone. I had to do a stunt in her place. The trouble was that they had my signature on the dotted line as agreeing to the terms and conditions. When I found out what the stunt entailed, I came within an ace of walking out right there and then. Breach of contract or not.

It appeared that I was to be lowered encased in a sort of glass coffin, into a tank of water and remain submerged there for a total of thirty seconds!!

If that doesn`t seem too bad, try timing yourself holding your breath for that length of time. The only thing that kept me on set was the thought of all that lovely money I had been offered to take the job in the first place. It really was an enormous sum by contemporary standards. Perhaps I should have smelt a rat before I signed the contract. I don`t know. Anyway in for a penny in for a pound. I was going to give it my best go. Although I was quite an accomplished swimmer and reasonably happy in the water rather than afraid of it, I can`t claim to be an especially brave person. I was really wound up with apprehension, and the first few rehearsals were quite disastrous. I did nothing but choke, and must have swallowed quite a few gallons in the process. My salvation came when somebody suggested that things would almost certainly improve if I were to bung up my ears and my nose with cotton wool. This was rather uncomfortable as well, but I soon got used to it, and it was certainly the lesser of the two evils. By the time we had another few rehearsals under our belts, I was much happier about the whole thing. I was also continuing to think about the money involved and just what I would be able to do with it, and it steeled my resolve.

When everybody had pronounced themselves happy with the rehearsals I was sent to the West End to be fitted with my costume for the scene. This was exactly the same as Simone`s outfit, consisting only of a pink satin one piece swimsuit. This was in the days before the bikini took the limelight. The swimsuit was trimmed with shells and pearls and there was a lovely spangled net cloak to go over me. A flowered headdress completed the outfit. It wasn`t the sort of thing you could pick up off the peg at Marks and

Sparks, and therefore the fitting was to take place at a particularly exclusive London couturiers who were designers and fitters to the stars. The salon was fitted out with the sort of opulence for which the word "luxury" is totally inadequate. It was a different world. As I entered I was greeted by two beautiful Borzoi dogs which were a part of the salon`s image and certainly not there as guard dogs or anything like that! They were perfectly groomed and well trained, in addition to being especially well fed, so they contented themselves with giving me a thorough sniffing rather than taking a bite.

During my fitting which took rather a long time considering the small number of garments involved, the assistant told me that Margaret Lockwood was being dressed in the adjoining cubicle. Margaret was at the pinnacle of her career at that time, and along with countless others I`m sure, I idolised her, and hoped that I might get a chance of a peep before I had finished at the salon but I was disappointed unfortunately. Just another one of my frustrated ambitions.

Simone October 1946 filming Temptation Harbour

Work on my own particular part of the film lasted for a total of about four weeks, during which time it would have been impossible for me to travel every day. We had to be on set really early in the morning, so the answer was to look for somewhere to stay fairly close by. I was extremely lucky in having a friend living in the area, so I moved in with her for the filming period. Her name was Moira Redmond. She was just beginning to make her mark as an actress at the time, and I`m delighted to see that she`s still a trouper, having taken a major role in a TV play not so very long ago.

For my own personal scenes in this minor epic I had to stand at the side of the glass coffin. My cloak and headdress were removed by someone standing behind me. I had to step into the coffin with an enormous smile, as if I were enjoying the whole thing and lie down with my hands crossed over my chest. A bit too much like a corpse I thought! Then two of the actors picked up the coffin and lowered it and me into the water tank. I can`t remember who took the foot end but the actor at my head was the wonderfully talented and sadly missed Robert Newton. Just like Margaret Lockwood he seemed to be in every single film being made at that time.

Now comes the explanation of what this stunt was all about. The film contained a sort of subplot involving a circus act known as "The Disappearing Mermaid." Perhaps I was lucky that they didn`t want to fit me out with a fish-tail! The coffin was lowered into the tank which was made of glass so the audience could see exactly what was going on. (Or so they thought anyway.) After my immersion, curtains were drawn around and nothing much happened for the next thirty seconds except for the build-up of tension and my face turning puce in colour. After that time the coffin was hauled up and the curtains drawn back and Hey Presto! The mermaid had disappeared. We managed to get the scene in the can after only three takes, which was quite good. In between takes I was wrapped in towels immediately. My costume being made of pink satin, became virtually transparent when wet, so it looked for all the world as if I were standing there in the nude! I might have been a Windmill Girl and all that, but I still had my modesty and the towels really were a Godsend. My costume and I also had to be thoroughly dried out in between takes for obvious reasons.

At the end of the day or more accurately the four weeks, everyone involved thought that things had gone particularly well. The crew and technicians, my fellow actors and the director couldn`t have been nicer or more helpful. Even the great Simone Simon herself who had a fearsome reputation as a tartar and was notoriously difficult to work with was kind and charming towards me. I ended up liking her immensely. Naturally cynics will say that she had to be as nice as pie to me as I was the only person who stood between her and the tank of water. I`m certain she wouldn`t have wanted to do the thing for herself. Among the other interesting happenings whilst I was on set I was thrilled to meet the quite famous Mischa Spolianski who had written the delightful music for the film, and to share my meal breaks with Irene Handl, who was always such an enjoyable companion. Irene was a seasoned performer, full of interesting stories and always ready to pass on little tips which she herself had learned in the hard school of experience. I`ve often had cause to value those all too brief sessions with her, and always felt a thrill of pride whenever I saw her on TV.

Filming finished, incredibly, quite close to schedule on a Friday afternoon and we were due to start rehearsals at the Windmill on the following Monday. A whole precious weekend in which to relax and gear myself up to a bit of positive thinking. A fair bit of cash in the bank helped my thoughts to run on pleasant lines and Mother`s condition had remained on a sort of plateau, so I didn`t have to concern myself too much in that direction. Mother was enjoying her new lease of life tremendously, and Father was home every night to spoil her just a little bit. Perhaps most important of all, I had the wherewithal to repay Dad`s generous loan of eighty quid, and lost no time in doing so.

CHAPTER NINE

The Windmill

Pat and I turned up at the theatre in plenty of time for rehearsals on the Monday and found that management had allowed two full weeks for rehearsals. Quite enough time to smooth off the corners and rough edges before the show was due to start. All the girls it appeared were pretty well experienced. Some of them had been around for quite a while longer than Pat or me, and a few of them had been appearing at the Windmill right through the whole of the War, during which time the theatre adopted the slogan "We Never Closed" and said so with pride on every appropriate occasion. It didn`t take too long therefore before we all came to understand exactly what was required of us, and the show began to take meaningful shape quite quickly. Both choreographer and Dance arranger, Keith and Maisie I`d already met as they were present at my original audition. Both were extremely talented folk and perfectionists to boot. As they had every right to be.

In addition to the actual mechanics of the dances for the show, we were subjected to the tender care of the wardrobe mistress and her gang, who took innumerable sets of measurements to make certain that our costumes would fit us perfectly. This occurred during the first couple of days of rehearsals so that they could be sure that the costumes would be ready in plenty of time. Mr. Van Damm, who amazingly enough preferred to be known as V.D. (!!) was very keen to be able to inspect us in full rig-out well before the starting date of the show, ideally before the end of the first week of rehearsal. When I saw my costume I was horrified! Obviously I wasn`t expecting to be rigged out as a crinoline lady, but this little lot was really something. It came to only just a bit more than a g-string and a few square inches of net. Back to my mermaid episode and looking as if I were unclad! Still I`d signed on the dotted line again, and whatever it was, it was better than the Dole. More seriously, I valued the challenge as well as the prospect of quite a fat pay packet and at least I was within reasonable reach of home rather than having to live out of suitcases in a succession of filthy digs all the time. Pat was in the same boat, as she was then living with her parents somewhere out Dagenham way, and we were both able to travel each way by tube and trolleybus without too many problems.

On the Sunday, the day before the show was due to open, we had the final dress rehearsal, perhaps a bit ironically named in view of the scanty nature of the dress. Parents, relatives and /or special friends could be invited to this as a sort of free preview. I asked my Mother and Dad to come with some misgivings because I didn`t know how they would react to seeing their dear daughter, in fact, seeing rather more of her than they had been accustomed to in the past. My worries were groundless as it happened. At the end Mother remarked how much she had enjoyed the show and said that she thought the costumes were really beautiful. I found out much later that because of the very clever way in which the lighting was arranged and operated, the whole thing looked very artistic indeed and not at all "rude."

The Lord Chamberlain`s merry men called at the theatre, as they had used to do when we worked the provinces, but somebody, somewhere must have tipped off the Windmill management that the "spies" were on their way. On these occasions we girls would receive a message over the Tannoy, just saying "Knickers WILL be worn for tonight`s performances." Wardrobe department supplied the appropriate garments, which were themselves quite brief and scanty, but "We wore`em with decorum" and everybody was happy. At least I don`t recall any prosecutions during that period.

At this time I still used my given name, and was therefore known to everybody as Joan. This got a bit complicated because there were several other girls with the same name in the show at the time, and many people were forever getting mixed up between us all. Usually it all ended up by everyone having a laugh about it, but such confusion could have caused a lot of lost time, something which always seemed to be in short supply at the "Mill." Eventually V.D. decided that it would be better if we reduced the number of Joans by at least one, and suggested that it would be a good idea to call me Simone as a sort of reminder of my cinematic adventure. "We shouldn`t have too much trouble with you having THAT name!" he said. I was of course, quite happy to fall in with his wishes. A change of name is not a particularly important item, and I broke the news gently to Mother and Dad, who accepted the matter perfectly well. I was still their "little Joanie" I suppose, so what other folk called me didn`t really matter too much to them. Apart from Joan, there was another name which seemed to be very popular among many of my friends, acquaintances and fellow artistes, and that was Pat. Throughout my life I have known ever so many girls with that name, and I can honestly say that practically all of them were really nice people, always friendly and helpful. Perhaps I`ve just been lucky but there must be some bitchy Pats about somewhere after all. One of the Pats I remember so well across the years was Pat Raphael. She was an extremely pretty girl being half Chinese, with classic Eurasian features and a lovely figure. As I recall she returned to her childhood home in Singapore, which she had been fortunate enough to have left before the Japanese invasion. As well as being so wonderfully endowed by Nature, Pat also possessed a lot of ambition and many talents. We heard that she had opened her own nightclub in the city and from the reports which came back to us every now and again it seemed that she was doing rather nicely thank you! I do hope that things all turned out well for her, because there are all too many illustrations of how tough the nightclub business can be and Pat certainly deserved at least a reasonable return for all the hard work and money she had invested in her business.

The Pat who was my original friend and tap-dancing coach and who had joined the Windmill at the same time as me was Pat Hamilton. She was still living at home, out near Dagenham at this time, but we often recalled the interminable days and nights in grotty digs, when we talked for hours, mainly because there was nothing else to do. There was no TV outside London and in any case, the type of accommodation which suited our pockets didn`t even run to a radio in one`s room, let alone anything more sophisticated. We didn`t have the time or the inclination to go out to the cinema, and we certainly didn`t want to be seen as the type of girls who went to pubs. Women who went pubbing without a male escort in those days were usually tarty types on the lookout for business. The other major pastime was dancing, and we had quite enough of that, thank you. In any case, with two shows a night plus matinees and rehearsal time, all our leisure hours such as they were, occurred during the day, when activities were much more restricted.

Pat had lots of interesting stories to tell about her early life. She`d started on the stage at a much more tender age than I had, being an accomplished child performer. She`d been helped and encouraged all along the way by her mother, who travelled around with her and accompanied her songs and dances on the piano. She remarked that her Father was very much older than her

Mum and was almost a grandfather figure to Pat herself. He took little or no active interest in her performances, being content to back her up from a distance as it were. The setup didn`t seem to have affected her in any way. She always struck me as being a particularly well balanced and happy go lucky sort of character. Having said that, however, I often got the impression that talking to me helped her overcome her homesickness. When she went on tour as a child, she`d always had Mum on hand, but now that she was on her own, it`s quite possible that she felt a bit lonely and "down." The advantage I had in this respect was that I was well seasoned in the idea of living away from home. I`d had to come to terms with it during my ATS days. The main difference between service life and our more recent existence in digs, was that the ATS always made sure you were reasonably well fed and for free!

In spite of being aware of the advantages of living at home, we did have a couple of small problems about travelling which started to become obvious some time after we started appearing in the show. The last performance usually finished at an hour which gave us reasonable time to change, remove surplus make-up and catch the Tube or Trolleybus, getting us home at a not too disreputable hour. However, there was always the possibility of encountering some of the few odd-bods who were about at night even then, and there were one or two incidents that caused us a little concern. I discussed the topic with some of the other girls and decided we`d be a bit better off and probably safer if we shared a flat nearer the theatre. Before too long, a chance came along and we grabbed it. The flat was in Bedford Court Mansions, not too far away, but the "Mansions" bit must have been added by some Estate Agent or other. Someone with a vivid imagination. Still, it was roomy, very comfortable and reasonably priced. In any case, we were earning quite generous salaries by then and could afford to be a bit choosy. After quite a lot of discussion, Pat eventually decided to continue travelling nightly with the proviso that there would be a place for her to crash out if she ever needed to. The flat was quite big enough for us to be able to put up the occasional guest. This left me with a couple of excellent flatmates called Lisa and Joan. Joan worked as a secretary in a nearby office (Poor thing!). We all got on very well together sharing all the chores as equally as we could. During all our time together, I can remember only one real disaster and that was my fault. It was my turn to do the cooking and we had already started to experiment with herbs and spices in the hope of producing something good and tasty. Our memories of the dreaded POM were still quite strong! The herb of the month as it were, was garlic, so I added it to my offering without a second thought. BIG trouble! I must have seriously miscalculated the quantity because we all went down with nasty tummy problems. I was careful after that, believe me.

One of the few drawbacks to living in "London Proper" was that every Sunday was dreary and dreadful, with absolutely nothing going on. Because of this, it was a welcome relief to be able to go home to the family for Sunday. At least it gave me a chance to catch up on some of the more everyday sort of stories which didn`t revolve around theatres and showbiz.

In spite of the hectic pace of our performances at the Windmill, we always made time to snatch the odd cuppa and have a bit of a gossip behind the scenes. Most of the girls got on pretty well with each other under the paternal eye of V.D. who took his responsibilities as a sort of surrogate father very seriously. He discouraged liaisons between "his" girls and their admirers (the stage door Johnnies), as he preferred to staff his shows with young unattached girls. In that way, I imagine, he wouldn`t have anybody failing to turn up through family difficulties. The only exception to this rule, at least as far as I can remember was yet another Joan, Her married name was Joan Keen, and she`d already been married for quite a while before I got to know her. Another unusual facet of this particular Joan was that she was the only one of us whom Jimmy Edwards, who was our resident comedian at that time, could be bothered to speak to. Our "Head Girl" at the "Mill" was Joan Jay, a very beautiful brunette who played at the theatre during the war years and had sustained injuries by shrapnel. She was a wonderful dancer and I was always fascinated to watch from the side of the stage when the opportunity arose to see her slow developer. This was an unfolding of the leg which, without any effort used to end up behind her ear! The times I wished I could be as supple as her. There were several girls at the "Mill" called Joan. Joan Kent whose talents V.D. did not appreciate too much, proved him wrong when she made her way into films and became a star. Another name which will be familiar to many especially film fans, was Hazel Court. She left us quite soon after Pat and I joined and went from strength to strength carving herself quite a distinguished career in films during the forties and early fifties. Another girl who became famous but for VERY different reasons, was Christine Welsford. After leaving the theatre she put on an enormous amount of weight quite quickly, so much so in fact that she ended up very much in demand as one of the foremost outsize models of the day. Perhaps because dancing under hot lights burns up so many calories, she couldn`t come to terms with having to adjust her food intake when her strenuous lifestyle altered. Who Knows! One of the nudes was courted by a gentleman called Val Guest. His was a particularly well-known name then especially in showbiz circles and I can`t remember whether he produced or directed shows. He might have even done both I suppose. He ended up married to his ex-nude. There was certainly a romance between them, which had gone on for quite a while.

Night in and night out as we danced and sang. Most of us were quite young and had limited experience of the world, so perhaps we weren`t aware of the importance of what we were doing in the psychological sense. Britain just after the war was quite a grim place, with rationing still in force; acres of bombed sites all over the place; a very limited choice of goods in most shops and a general air of "What on Earth did we think we were fighting for" on the part of many ex-service personnel. The sad part is that a lot of this type of attitude was fully justified. Our dancing and songs, I`m sure, helped just a little to mask the unpleasant realities of life in the austerity of the mid-Forties. Odd thing memory isn`t it? The pictures or most of them, from over seventy years ago, are still crystal clear. But don`t ask me what I had for breakfast yesterday.

One of the faces and figures I remember from those days, was a girl called Wanda, who was the daughter of a professor. Anita D`Ray, (whose father DIDN`T drive for a brewery!) became the focus of a lot of juicy gossip following her marriage. We all thought she had landed a good catch when she walked down the aisle with the owner of the famous Skindles restaurant in Maidenhead. Everybody who wanted to be noticed and to be featured in the glossies HAD to dine at Skindles in those days. Good for Anita we thought. Hubby isn`t short of a bob or two. Sad to relate and an illustration that cash doesn`t always buy happiness, the marriage proved a total mis-match very soon after they`d tied the knot. The inevitable divorce ensued, an awful lot of dirty linen was washed, and the full gory details were paraded with great relish by the more sensational newspapers of the time. There weren`t any tabloids as such, but the type of people who write for the gutter press have always been with us. In any case, we hadn`t really begun to copy the U.S. fashion for "rubber stamp" divorces. Annulments in the post-war period involved a long drawn out legal battle, with all the full circus of the law having a field day. Divorce certainly wasn`t for the faint-hearted or those a bit short of cash.

Lisbeth Kearns a well-known name especially to aficionados of musical theatre and Vicki Emra, whose speciality leaned more towards Flamenco and other rather more exotic classical Spanish Dances were able to attract good audiences and were obviously doing very nicely thank you when it came to cash in the bank and fine clothes.

These were the days when the Windmill was at its peak, enjoying a world-wide reputation. Quite aside from our civilian customers, the theatre had become a "Must See" for large numbers of servicemen of all types and from all corners of the world, who were stationed over here, or just passing through. News of its wonders was then spread by word of mouth. No doubt with some embellishments when these chaps returned home. In spite of this household name situation the theatre was if anything rather too small and cramped for comfort. Strict and careful choreography and discipline were essential in order to avoid collisions or other mishaps on the quite tiny stage.

Another factor which could quite easily have led to disaster was the presence of a number of glass plates set flush with the surface of the stage and covering various sorts of lamps. These differed in colour and intensity, and were used for some of the clever lighting effects which were characteristic of our shows. These plates were a potential death trap, with the ever-present danger of slipping as it was impossible to avoid them. To combat this we had special rubber tips fitted to our shoes, which made us feel a lot more secure. I wonder if the plates have survived, given today`s climate of Health and Safety at work. Still, I suppose there must be a little bit of leeway allowed somewhere, and there`s no escaping the fact that these plates and the lamps underneath helped to produce some stunning lighting effects. They were really avant-garde in our days of some seventy years back, but perhaps like so many other things they`ve been superseded since. Who knows?

Quite apart from the girls names who I`ve already mentioned, the theatre provided a sort of nursery or starting off point for a vast number of other showbiz folk whose names have since taken their place amongst the best known in the country. Most of them were the fill-in comedians, like Jimmy Edwards; Harry Secombe; Alfred Marks; Arthur English and Bruce Forsyth, who came on to provide a sort of breathing space for changes of costumes and/or scenery. Many of the predominantly male audiences regarded these poor fellows as a total waste of time and the job of the Windmill comic was NOT an easy one. The comedians and some other acts who came into the shows from time to time worked from scripts prepared for them, and the scriptwriters at the Mill when I started were a pair of young fresh-faced lads called Frank Muir and Denis Norden. Further comment from me is unnecessary, I`m sure! They were of course, fresh out of the Forces and just starting to find their feet in showbiz at that time, but were still responsible for a very large number of extremely funny and well-written shows. In addition to the scriptwriters the theatre also employed a songwriter, the dance-arranger Maisie, and the choreographer Keith, so we were pretty well self-contained. All the staff were well aware of the restrictions imposed by the size of the theatre and stage and we all worked very closely together as a tightly knit team.

Administration was taken care of by a couple of offices where a couple of girls banged away at typewriters. I can`t say I was ever taken by nostalgia when I saw them at work! There was also a Publicity Office, responsible for all the photographs taken within the theatre, which often amounted to quite considerable numbers. Cameras in the audience were strictly forbidden. A sudden unexpected photoflash could have led to serious accidents during dance routines etc. All the official photographic apparatus was also stored in the Publicity Office, carefully under lock and key, as it was bang up-to-date and very expensive.

Costumes were designed and made on the premises, within a small but very professionally run wardrobe department, which also took care of the more mundane work like laundry and running repairs etc. Work here was carried out under the eagle eye of the Costume Designer/Wardrobe Mistress who, just like all the other members of staff set high standards and ensured that they were followed by her entourage. The remaining backstage space was taken up by a small canteen. Right at the top of the building were our dressing rooms and of course, the Green Room, which we used as a sort of social lounge, a hospitality room or just somewhere we could relax. The dressing rooms were quite a bit better than we used to find at many provincial theatres. There were good sized mirrors and plenty of lighting, which helped us in making up before shows. I watched points as best I could and picked up innumerable tips from the other girls, to the extent that I became quite an accomplished makeup artist. This skill stood me in very good stead much later on, when I returned to the stage after some years of absence. Last but by no means least, came the music department. The size of the theatre ruled out our having any sort of orchestra, so all our shows were accompanied by two pianists and a drummer. They always coped very well with a vast repertoire and a selection of music from Back to Boogie. But I don`t suppose for a moment their talent and versatility were appreciated by the audience. Basically the nightly punters paid to sit there and drool over scantily clad or even unclad crumpet and anything else was a total irrelevance.

Pictures of the Windmill Theatre

Simone as Simone Grew, at the Windmill Theatre, 1945

At the Windmill Theatre

Revudeville Souvenir, featuring Simone, 1947

At the Windmill Theatre, London

At the Windmill, Pat and I soon found that we were not alone in our sun-worshipping interests. Several of the other girls were always very happy to join us on fine days in a general rush to the roof, where we could sunbathe in comparative seclusion. Like most nice things, it didn`t last. The rebuilding of London was well under way by now, and bombed sites were being cleared and redeveloped everywhere. Before we properly realised just what was going on, we were being overlooked by beefy builders hanging from scaffolding like so many orangutans and wolf whistling until their teeth rattled. We started off by being a bit annoyed, not to say outraged, but soon realised that it was all meant as bit of good clean fun. After all, we were showgirls, not frumps, and they wouldn`t have whistled if they hadn`t found us attractive. It was quite a sincere compliment in its own way, I suppose, so we waved, smiled and carried on as if nothing was happening. Today`s girls would probably have whistled back, but the thought never occurred to us.

Life at the Windmill was almost an echo of schooldays in some respects. Discipline was sometimes quite severe and V.D. ruled with an iron rod. He kept a strict eye on us in more ways than one as well. He did actually have an annoying habit of walking straight into our dressing rooms without knocking, often finding some of us with nothing on. We were aware that he was a family man. His daughter Sheila Van Damm, was to become a world-beating motor racing driver a few years after this, but nonetheless he was still a man who should never have been allowed in the girls dressing rooms at all. Many of the girls adopted a bit of a blasé attitude about it all, but I for one never quite got used to this habit of his. He discouraged boy/girl relationships amongst the company`s personnel and put all the local dance halls firmly out of bounds to us. It was well known that he had actually sacked two girls some time previously, just because they broke the no dance hall rule, so this made quite certain that the rest of us would toe the line without demur.

Keith Lester our Dance Arranger/Choreographer was amongst the highest in his profession at this time, and it was sheer delight to work with him. Although he demanded nothing short of sheer perfection, we were aware that he was well able to carry out the routines for himself and never asked the impossible. He chose beautiful and evocative music for all the ballets and tableaux he staged, and I`m quite certain that I have Keith to thank for much of the pleasure that good music has given me ever since those days. Keith`s selections enabled me to appreciate for the first time the delicate and quite ethereal beauty of Debussy, although he was perfectly happy to use works by Rossini; Friedemann; Strauss; Delibes; Tchaikovsky and Coleridge Taylor. It`s far from likely that many of the audience would have appreciated his musical choice. The Windmill was much more a place for exercising the eyes and the imagination. Apparently, it wasn`t uncommon to have chaps standing in a queue for several hours, just to be certain of grabbing a centre seat, front row. In fact, one chap, so the story goes, fighting to get to the front centre seat, actually broke his neck, and died! I can`t see what advantage could be gained by being at the front, as the theatre was very small and intimate, and all seats commanded a pretty good view anyway.

Keith Lester was a very handsome man and his constant dancing and practice had helped him maintain a fine figure. His presence was something good and positive. You always had the impression that if you were really prepared to have a go, then Keith would move heaven and earth to help you out and back you fully. When we first saw him at practice class, however, practically every one of us collapsed with a fit of the giggles. Keith`s costume consisted of a vest, bright cerise tights and a matching sweat band. A somewhat unusual sight in those days, even for a ballet dancer. He was obviously well ahead of his time in the fashion stakes.

There were odd occasions when things happened to make us question some aspects of V.D.`s attitude and motivation. He was certainly happy to pose as some sort of father figure, but he could be quite cruel, almost sadistic on occasions. He expected unquestioning obedience to his orders, as was the norm, but sometimes it seemed as if he enjoyed going over the top, just to be awkward. He told Lisa, on one occasion, who, as well as being my flatmate and also one of my best friends, that she`d have to do a solo tap item in one of the shows, springing this on her at terribly short notice. Almost in tears, poor Lisa stammered, "But V.D. I`ve never done tap in my life. I trained in classical ballet." This was perfectly true. Before joining us at the Mill, Lisa had been a member of the quite famous Anglo-Polish Ballet Company. He shrugged off her objections, totally unperturbed. "Well, be that as it may, you`ll just have to get on and do it." As it turned out she gritted her teeth, made the best of a bad job and actually succeeded in producing a very competent and polished performance on the night. A couple of us waded in and helped her. I`d been put in a very similar spot by the Sherman-Fisher episode, so I obviously understood exactly how she felt.

The musical side of our shows usually included a few songs, and several of the girls had very good voices. I can`t really claim to have been any sort of prima donna, although I wasn`t too unhappy to do the odd solo singing spot. This hadn`t always been the case though because some years previously my father of all people remarked on one occasion that he didn`t like my singing voice. It didn`t impress him at all and he thought I`d be better off concentrating on dancing. All the same I decided that there was no harm in making certain, and that it would help my morale and confidence if I were to take some singing lessons. There was a good singing trainer fairly near the theatre, so I signed up there and went along for coaching in the songs from our various shows. Our resident comedian at this time was Alfred Marks, who was also studying with the same teacher and we used to go along together for our lessons. Alfred had the most wonderful rich bass voice and it was a real treat to be able to listen in to his lessons. He was also an excellent comedian, and kept us in stitches with his stories, both on and off the stage. He was part of a line-up of comedians over the years, which included such names as Harry Secombe, Arthur English and Gus Chevalier.

I`d kept up my friendship with Dennis, right through the War years, although it was never anything more than platonic. The old cliché, `just good friends` sums it up neatly. As well as keeping my friendship, Dennis had also succeeded in holding on to "Poppet." She was still in amazingly good condition for her age. They certainly built them to last in those days! A few bits had been added and a few others had fallen off, but she was still driveable and capable of giving us an awful lot of fun. Dennis and his friend Laurie used to call at the theatre regularly to collect Pat and me, and we used to make up a foursome. It must have looked a bit odd to say the least having two hulking great blokes crammed into that tiny car, hiding Pat and me almost completely. Laurie was quite tall, and his head actually touched Poppet`s roof. On one specially memorable occasion, the boys turned up, to find the whole side street jam-packed with other cars. Nothing daunted, Dennis and Laurie picked up Poppet carried her sideways and placed her neatly between two great limousines. It was a tight fit, but they made it, and we all had a terrific laugh about it. It`s so true that you never have a camera handy on such occasions. Sometimes when we went out after dark although not infrequently, as we had a show to complete first. I`d be given the job of holding a cycle lamp out of the side window, as there was usually something askew with dear old Poppet`s lighting circuit. Laurie was, in turn, responsible for holding out and blowing on an ancient bulb-horn when we went around corners. This was the only practical way of our giving warning of our approach. Oh the follies of youth, not to mention the blessings of not having any form of MOT test in those days. One tangible benefit of all our outings in the car was that Pat and Laurie began to develop deeper and deeper feelings for each other. Eventually they decided that they were sufficiently in love to take the plunge and ended up happily married. As for Dennis and me, well that`s quite another story with a very different outcome.

At this time the shows we were staging at the Windmill all followed the same basic format. Apart from minor alterations to the music, they consisted of dancing girls; a couple of songs interspersed here and there; a comedian; a nude tableau; more dancing girls etc. etc. It was quite hard work for us dancers, but generally speaking we enjoyed what we were doing, and the predominantly male clientele seemed perfectly happy with our efforts. We played to packed houses night after night. Another factor on the plus side was that the money was very good. Things went along quite well for a considerable time, and I`d really found my feet at the theatre - or so I thought. I was pulled up sharply however, when V.D. called me into his office and told me in so many words that he was firing me forthwith. "I`ve noticed for some time that you aren`t doing any high kicks, and I know why. This sort of false modesty is no good for this theatre. It`s time you got used to wearing these costumes and remembered that the entertainment we provide is mainly for male audiences. If you are going to suffer any sort of embarrassment, then you aren`t going to be much good here. You`d better leave and look for something more suitable." He was dead right in his surmise. I WAS more than a bit embarrassed, so I had no real answer to give him. I packed my bags, bade a tearful farewell to Pat and a few of the other girls and off I went. As a generous parting gesture V.D. invited me to attend a party which was being held to mark the theatre`s anniversary. There was a special show to mark the occasion as well, but I was barred from appearing in it. Perhaps if I`d known what was to happen at the party and the total upheaval it was to produce in my life, I might not have been so pleased to have the invitation, in fact, and with the benefit of hindsight, it`s most likely that I would have run a mile in the opposite direction. Still we don`t know these things at the time, do we?

A couple of days went by and I had some time to think about my situation. The more I mulled things over, the more annoyed I became, until I began to consider that V.D. had done me a real, deep injustice. I determined that I was going to make a really big splash at the party and that, if I was going to go down, then I would do so with all guns firing, as it were. I went shopping with serious determination, and ended up spending quite a lot more than I could really afford. For my money, I ended up with a really super creation - a stunning number in gold lame, which fitted like a second skin and showed off my figure to perfection. At the risk of blowing my own trumpet, I must admit that I had an excellent figure at the time. My dancing kept me fit and shapely, and I also exercised quite a bit. To go with the posh frock, I went to a rather exclusive, upmarket salon to get my hair properly sorted out. This also cost me more than I could afford, but the end result made it all worthwhile. This question of a super hairdo was a little bit of a dig at V.D. In fact, he paid the hairdressing expenses for those girls he particularly fancied, but the rest of us had to fork out from our own pockets. I aimed to show him that we could produce just as good results off our own bats as came out of the swish salons he or rather his lady friends patronised. I don`t know if this succeeded, but at least he didn`t have any room to criticise my hair, something he had done more than once in the past. To go with my hair and outfit, I took particular care with my make-up and spent ages manicuring myself. It was a real luxury to be able to take time in front of the mirror. We usually had a frantic rush to get changed and made up in time to get on stage during shows, but of course, the audience was never any wiser about this.

I made the grandest entrance I possibly could and quite a number of heads turned as I sashayed past. I hugged myself inside when I saw for certain that my ploy was successful. I really had knocked old V.D. for six! He looked me over and with a complete departure from his usual attitude, he complimented me quite profusely on my appearance. Even then though he couldn`t resist the chance to be totally patronising, remarking "I think you have learned your lesson. Report for rehearsals on Monday week." I was overjoyed at this bit of news. I suppose it was in the nature of a bit of a climb down for V.D. I really looked forward to rejoining my gang of truly great friends behind the footlights. The party had been tremendously well organised, and was a fabulous "do" from every point of view. I danced until I could dance no more. There was a terrific band who really knew how to get everyone`s feet tapping. One of my partners was Stirling Moss, then at the height of his fame as a world beating racing driver. Apart from the music and dancing, there was an enormous buffet, with eats and drinks of every kind imaginable. I thought "To Hell with any sort of diet. This is once in a lifetime," and got well stuck in to the wonderful food. I sampled a couple of the more exotic drinks as well, but didn`t find anything really special or exciting in the booze line.

Very early television performance by 12 of the Windmill Girls (1945-6)

CHAPTER TEN

Meeting David

Whilst I was there with my lower jaw going at a rate of knots, a smartly-dressed middle-aged man came over and engaged me in a fascinating conversation. I really can`t remember any of the topics we discussed, but I recall being totally enthralled by him. He had a pleasant soft voice. He introduced himself as David, and admitted frankly that he`d come to the party in the hope of seeing Lesley, who was one of the nudes. Naturally she had some clothes on at the party. David said that he was a regular patron at the Windmill and had been admiring Lesley from the audience for some time. I didn`t really know her, because we girls split into two camps at the theatre. We were either nudes or dancers, and there wasn`t a great deal of mixing between us. As the conversation progressed it became more and more obvious that David had made up his mind to forget all about Lesley and he attached himself quite firmly to me for the rest of the evening. Among many other topics he told me that he was awaiting a decree nisi from his wife, whom he described as the Hon. Selina Clegg Hill, making it quite obvious that any affection between them had long since evaporated. It was only some considerable time later that I found out that David and Selina had only stayed together for about one year. Apparently they were joint Masters of a pack of hunting hounds and this interest in ritualistic killing was about all they had in common. It appears that life shortly became one endless row, and he decided that it would help his own peace of mind if he were to give her grounds for a divorce. At the time of the party his marital state was only referred to in the vaguest of terms and in any case, it was a matter which didn`t really interest me at all.

Whilst all this chatting up was going on, the normal end of the party signs were beginning to make themselves obvious. David eventually looked around at all the open spaces and accumulated litter, and suggested that we might go along to a night club to finish off the evening with a flourish. Although we`d talked for what seemed like ages, and he was a very likeable chap, I was all too aware that we had only met that evening and was just a little bit wary about accepting his invitation. I looked around for a possible chaperone, and saw another friend, Moira Redmond, who agreed to accompany us. Moira had been my sort of landlady during the filming episode at Welwyn, and was by now starting to become famous in her own right, starring in some major films and stage shows. Anyway, it was kind of her to agree on the spur of the moment like that, so off we went as a threesome.

This was the start of something really big! David became my own regular stage door Johnnie, bringing me flowers and presents of marron glaces from Fortnum and Mason. This delicacy was a particular favourite of mine, though usually well beyond my means, so I was really pleased at the way David pandered to my taste for luxury items as he did. It was quite a while before he came home with me to meet my parents, who were more than a little perturbed to learn that he was a full twenty four years older than I was and still technically a married man. V.D. also as soon as he found out, made sure of having his own say, sort of in loco parentis perhaps, telling me that I was all sorts of a damn fool to be going out with a man old enough to be my father. I wouldn`t listen however, and David and I seemed to be quite content to drift along accepting that we`d get married sooner or later, after his decree absolute had come through. This step would mean my leaving the Windmill but at least I had embarked on a truly worthwhile relationship. Wedding bells would mean a whole new and happy life for little me. Or so I thought at the time anyway.

David Lloyd-Davies, Grenadier Guards

I`d given a sort of open ended notice to V.D. and he agreed to let me appear in shows until a definite date for our marriage could be fixed. One of my numbers in the very last show before I left involved a vigorous Can-Can, including quite a lot of acrobatics. I wasn`t as supple as some of the other girls, so I found it essential to limber up with bending and stretching exercises before going on stage. This regime helped warm up my muscles so that I could cope with the flying splits which ended the dance. One evening I didn`t go through the routine. Total disaster followed. I went down for the splits as usual, but then found myself totally stuck and unable to get up again.

An ambulance was called and I was whisked off to Charing Cross Hospital where I ended up as a long term outpatient. It appeared that I`d done myself some considerable damage and it took a lot of expertise from the physiotherapists before I was pronounced cured and able to resume my rather energetic lifestyle. As well be imagined, V.D. was quite beside himself with rage, and made life so unpleasant that I decided I`d better finish immediately. I wasn`t too worried about this prospect, as my C.V. by then contained enough first-class background and experience to get me a worthwhile job almost anywhere. There were still plenty of live shows, so people like me could afford to be choosy about what we accepted. As it happened, I didn`t have to spend too much time looking around, because an offer came along within a couple of weeks. It involved my taking on a short season at a resort on the South Coast, to be followed immediately by a tour of British Service units stationed in Germany. This was organised by the Combined Services Entertainment Unit, and involved our putting on shows at a large number of Forces camps. Army and Air Force. These were scattered throughout the British Occupation Zone of Germany. When we went over, most of us took a selection of goodies hidden in our luggage. These included such items as coffee, sugar and chocolate, because we`d learned that the German people in general were even worse off than we were back home. We used these luxury items to barter for an amazing array of other goods and came back rather better off than we were on departure.

In spite of being reasonably well clued up because of what we`d heard and read about, we were unprepared for what we found on arrival. The actual conditions in Germany came as a terrific shock. People were literally scraping away in the ruins to salvage whatever they could find and the devastation in many places we visited was a lot worse than we`d experienced even in the badly hit parts of London.

During our tour, some of us being showgirls and therefore trying to look more glamorous than our sisters, decided to have a go at an idea for false eyelashes. These were commonplace and readily available in the States, but totally unknown in Europe at the time. We made up sets for ourselves using snippets of our own hair, stuck on strips of Elastoplast and fixed to our eyelids with stage gum. In spite of our collective skills in makeup etc., the whole episode was a disaster. As usual I was the fall guy. In the middle of one particularly energetic number the gum gave way on one side of my eye and a lump of horrible hairy gunge descended, blinding me effectively on one side, and making it look as if I were wearing a spider. Our false eyelashes ended up in the bin and nobody tried anything like it ever again. We just had to be patient and wait until the real McCoy became available over here. Only a couple of years later in fact. Although the original intention was that our show would tour Austrian bases after we`d completed our stint at the German ones, the show never really caught on with the troops for some reason. We packed up after about three months. Just in time to miss the winter sports. And came back to Blighty. A pleasant surprise awaited me in the form of a contract to do panto in Weymouth, so I signed on the dotted line immediately. There`s a small sting in the tail of the story of our German adventure. When we returned home, I was the only one out of the entire crowd to be grabbed by Customs and made to open my luggage. There was nothing in there. A bit ironic really, because most of the others who`d had more experience than I had were loaded down with Leica cameras and many other quite expensive items which they had bartered for coffee and chocolate.

While all this activity had been going on, and unknown to me, David`s decrees, both Nisi and Absolute had come through. Although he`d not bothered to tell me about this, he was rejoicing in his new status as a free, single man again. I`d better point out that I was not the "other woman" involved in David`s divorce. As I`ve already explained, he was almost half way through the proceedings when I first met him. I never asked him any questions about the actual "Third side of the Eternal Triangle," and he certainly never volunteered any information for himself. I decided it was far better to let sleeping dogs or rather sleeping partners lie, rather than risk a row. With the important bit of paper in his hand, David became keen for us to get married and my imminent departure on a panto date poured quite a lot of cold water on these particular little plans. He asked me a couple of times to break the date, but I pointed out that breach of contract proceedings would be bound to follow and hadn`t he spent enough cash to line lawyers pockets already? He had to see the sense of this, but got hold of a special licence anyway, saying that he wanted to get married as soon as possible, even if it meant postponing our honeymoon. There seemed to be a perverse sort of logic to this, but I agreed to go through with it and we were duly spliced at Ealing Registry Office on a bitterly cold December morning at the unearthly hour of 8.30 a.m. Naturally it wouldn`t have been practical for me to have insisted on a white wedding with all the trimmings, much as I would have loved to have had the chance. I got myself a smart two piece suit and was content. No coach-and-six or even a limousine for yours truly. My brother Norman and I travelled to the wedding by London Transport Trolleybus. Possibly due to the short notice involved, and in spite of all the close and bosom friends he claimed to have, David couldn`t come up with a best man and asked Norman to fill the post, which he did very effectively. The trolleybus stop was quite a distance from the Registry Office and Norman and I had rather a long dash to make to ensure we got there in good time. I`d barely got my breath back before having to gasp out the responses, but it all went well in the end. David and I had only a few hours together after the ceremony, as I had to catch a train to Weymouth at twelve noon. I suppose this cock-up was due to David. If he`d bothered to tell me in advance about the business of the Special Licence, or even the simple fact that his divorce was completed, I almost certainly wouldn`t have signed up for the Weymouth Panto. Nevertheless, they had my name on the dotted line, so that was it!

During our time in Weymouth, several of us used to spend some of our precious leisure hours in doing a bit of horse-riding in the glorious countryside in and around Exmoor. The horses were generally very docile and gave us no trouble. There was one outstanding exception. We`d stopped in a village to water the horses and I was busily in conversation with my next riding companion. I didn`t notice that my horse had lowered his head to drink. The next thing I realised was that I was sliding down his neck and over his head right into the pond! It was panto season in the bleak mid-winter, and the water was just a shade on the cool side. In addition it was a particularly muddy pond, and I struggled out caked from head to toe in sticky glutinous gunge. My hair was covered in a liberal coating and I could have gone on stage as the wicked witch with no help from make-up! My sympathetic companions roared their heads off at this edifying spectacle, and they were joined by many of the villagers who watched as I dripped my way back. To crown it all, we hadn`t really planned to do any riding that day, so we`d dressed up in our warmest clothes, slacks etc., on top of our pyjamas, in the hope that these layers would protect our legs and knees when riding. Because I was soaked, my slacks kept riding up to display my gaudy pyjama trouser legs underneath. It was quite a while before I was able to see the funny side of that little episode, I can assure you.

CHAPTER ELEVEN

Back Down To Earth

On my return home, David and I just sort of went from one day to the next in a very ordinary humdrum sort of way, and the question of our having any sort of honeymoon was never mentioned. Given David`s mean streak, perhaps it`s just as well for the sake of peace that I never insisted.

As it turned out, what I`d thought of as a step into connubial bliss actually led me straight from one pantomime into another very different one. Our marriage was tempestuous, to say the least right from the start. I always got the impression that David thought of our union as being totally Morganatic - the same as Edward VIII and Mrs. Simpson - in the way in which our social rankings differed. To be blunt he`d married beneath himself. It was a well-established truism that many marriages like this which sought to bridge class divisions were doomed to fail anyway. Certainly our married life was far from being a bed of roses for either of us I suppose. Coming from a lower middle class family, I was bound to come off worse, but I loved my Mum and Dad and respected the values they stood for. David and I had many arguments about this as he seemed to be obsessed with what he considered my pressing need for tuition and grooming. He wanted me to fit in with his "top-drawer" friends and the county types in whose company he considered himself at home. At this time, in fact, David spent his days in total idleness, scorning any type of meaningful occupation, and perfectly happy to describe himself as a "Gentleman of Leisure."

In case any further explanation is necessary, Edward Hanbury Carington David Lloyd-Davies, (He was fussy about the single `r` in Carington) who was a scion of a Welsh landowning family from way back, can only be described as a one hundred percent SNOB. As is often the case with such people, he had precious little of merit and virtually nothing of material worth to back up his pretentions. All the family members whom I actually met over the years were to say the least just a tiny bit eccentric, imbued with a totally false pseudo-Victorian sense of values with all the attendant hypocrisy. David himself was as it happens, a true Victorian having been born in 1898. How he and his relatives reconciled their family values with all the muck-raking and sordid gossip which must have accompanied David`s divorce was always a bit of a mystery to me. But then I suppose it was really none of my business.

Added to all this falsity it was obvious that David`s education had been a bit patchy considering that he had been educated by a private tutor. He had all the charm and social grace that came from a public school background, but his general knowledge was less than impressive. His Father was a great scholar. His Greek translations are still held in the archives of Rugby School where he was educated. I`m pretty sure that David`s Army career, also might not have borne too much examination, although he`d held a commission in both World Wars. For a chap with this sort of heavy commitment to King and Country, as it were, his collection of medals was a bit mediocre, both in quantity and quality, and the only thing I was able to gather about his career in WW2 was when he let something slip about being "attached" to M.I.6. As far as the Great War was concerned he did have a couple of shrapnel wounds in his arm and leg so he must have been somewhere close to the enemy at some time. They weren`t too serious and only gave him trouble on a couple of isolated occasions.

In spite of these upper-crust pretensions on the part of my new husband, he seemed perfectly happy for us to move in and live with my parents almost immediately after my return from Weymouth. The question of rent or any payment towards board and lodging was never mentioned and he appeared to be quite content at avoiding the need to part with his cash. The expression "hard-earned" certainly didn`t apply to him. What he did insist upon, however, and this REALLY DID upset me was that he should be treated as being more than just a cut above me and my family. One of his early moves was to present me with a book entitled "Lady Trowbridge`s Book of Etiquette" and to insist that I read it and act on its rules and precepts. Although my initial reaction was to regard this as a dreadful insult to me and mine, and to throw it straight back at him, I swallowed my resentment in the cause of peace and quiet, and made up my mind to at least have a go at pleasing this rather odd fellow.

Some months later it appears that David met up with an old Army friend who suggested in the course of conversation that some strings could be pulled to get David a job in the Foreign Office. He never told me exactly the whys and wherefores of what happened, but that was par for the course anyway. Because of his lack of qualifications, I don`t suppose the job itself was anything very grand, but it enabled him to play the ex-Officer, trot along to some mysterious office or other and sport his old Grenadier Guards tie. He would also be able to enjoy the company and fascinating anecdotes of his "peers." This made him reasonably happy. This enhancement of his status motivated David to decide on a move. A terraced house in Southall didn`t really match up to his new position, so it was decided by him that we should look for "An Address" which he considered to be a bit more suitable. There was no shortage of accommodation if you were prepared to pay a bit over the odds, so it wasn`t long before we found a flat vaguely in "The West End" and moved in.

CHAPTER TWELVE

Rillington Place

I was becoming more and more frustrated at living what was basically a life of idleness. I wasn`t cut out to be the little wifey in a pinny, up to her elbows in flour. What I really wanted was to get back behind the footlights, and stay fit and active. At the same time, although he obviously knew all about my background, David was not happy about my returning to the stage, as he regarded a showbiz career as rather infra-dig. My subscription to The Stage, was still in force, and I scanned the paper every week, just in case a really good offer came up which even David would find hard to make me turn down. Eventually as was bound to happen sooner or later, a particular advertisement caught my eye. It might have been worded especially for me, as it read: Wanted - a young shortsighted actress to take the lead in a documentary film. I applied straight away and got a reply in just over a week, inviting me for an audition. The address was a little bit off the beaten track and well away from the usual places where one found agent`s offices, but that didn`t necessarily mean anything. I discussed this possible leap into stardom with David and my parents. David was very grudging in his agreement, but eventually said I could go along and see what happened. My mother who had seen quite a few of my previous auditions come to nought, with the subsequent upsets, advised me to take Norman with me. Off we set, to find ourselves outside a tall, narrow and rather dingy house in a not too salubrious part of West London, Rillington Place. Norman left me on the doorstep, with an agreement to return in about fifteen to twenty minutes to collect me.

A tall, thin, smartly dressed man with receding hair and thick spectacles, answered the bell, welcomed me quite warmly, and led me up several flights of stairs. We eventually emerged onto a very shabby roof terrace, which seemed quite out of place as the setting for even a documentary film. Nevertheless I was aware that one should not judge by appearances, and snap decisions are not always the best guide either. The man was most charming, asking all sorts of questions about my background and career, seeming very interested in finding out whether I`d come to the audition on my own. I told him that my brother had escorted me and that he would very likely be waiting outside for me by this time. On hearing this, the man concluded my interview. We walked back down all those stairs to the street. Norman was in fact waiting there, and he bade us goodbye. I waited with growing disappointment for the result of my audition/interview and as the weeks lengthened, had resigned myself to having failed once again. Then one day, some weeks later, I picked up our daily paper, to see a familiar face staring out at me from the front page. It was my `film director` himself. My hands shook and icy shivers went through me as I read the accompanying story. I had been in the house of the Monster of Rillington Place - John Halliday Reginald Christie!! By the time I had met him he had already murdered at least six women and shoved their bodies behind a cupboard in his kitchen. God alone knows what would have happened to poor little me if I hadn`t taken Mother`s advice and had Norman along with me on that fateful day.

CHAPTER THIRTEEN

Baby On The Way

Nature being what it is and in spite of our marriage being a bit less than blissful, I found myself pregnant. David was not exactly delighted at this bit of news and immediately insisted that I had to get rid of the baby. To add insult to injury, he said that this little adventure was to be carried out at MY EXPENSE!! I did the rounds of the chemists shops over quite a wide area in my search to get something that would work. Totally without success of course. I obviously couldn`t tell the chemists exactly what I was trying to do, and the whole setup around abortions was highly illegal at that time, carrying heavy penalties. All I succeeded in doing was swallowing an obnoxious cocktail of drugs and purgatives which upset my system quite seriously.

At long last when he could see that I was still pregnant and going to stay that way, darling David reverted to being the patriotic Welshman insisting that his son must be born in Wales. The possibility of his siring a daughter never occurred to him for one second. The subject of my pregnancy was in fact one of the very few occasions where I beat him in an argument, but this was solely because I had, perhaps not surprisingly, a troublesome nine months and the upheaval of a move to Wales would have been far too much for me. As my time neared, it became essential for me to go into hospital for special care and David`s preferences had to go by the board. He did actually provoke several arguments with the medical staff, but common sense prevailed in the end, so our son - yes he was right about that - was actually born on the "wrong" side of Offa`s Dyke. We christened him Richard.

Simone with Richard, 1948

On my leaving hospital with our son and heir. At least that`s what I thought his status was going to be, we three returned to Southall to live with my parents again. In spite of having an extra mouth to feed David`s meanness with money was still very evident, and relations were quite fraught with constant arguments and some quite unpleasant scenes. He still had his job, with a salary coming in, but my parents and I saw very little of the contents of his wallet. In spite of my family`s obvious "social inferiority", David was quite happy to sponge off them quite shamelessly, until Dad`s patience finally ran out. He told my ever-loving quite frankly that it was time he realised that he now had dependants and that he needed to get himself together. This triggered another round of house hunting, but David`s snobbery was still the main motivation behind his choices, so he confined himself to looking only in the very best parts of London. We ended up in a small, pokey flat again vaguely in the West End and with an astronomical rent to find every week. Because of the huge strain this placed on our budget, our stay at the flat was not a very long one.

Another constant cause of fights and spats between us was David`s insistence that our son`s name was to be entered for Eton and Sandhurst. Please don`t ask me where he thought the money was going to come from. We couldn`t even manage the rent of our flat, for Goodness Sake! Apart from my own opposition, Nature again came out on my side to frustrate David`s ambition. Richard was far from enjoying the best of health, being plagued with very poor muscle tone and lack of co-ordination, and also suffering from a kind of asthma, which left him on occasion having to struggle and gasp for every breath. With hindsight, it`s more than possible that the inner city environment didn`t agree with him. A further factor which still haunts me over the years is that my attempts to abort Richard may well have had something to do with his subsequent ill health. I can`t help blaming myself and it has been difficult to live with my conscience ever since.

David's ambition for his son was crushed, a remark to his son one day which Richard has never forgotten was: "You are a failure and will never be able to make your own way in the world." It caused a rift between father and son.

Although the term "Smog" hadn`t been coined yet, we knew all about the phenomenon and some of its effects. The fogs of the late forties and early fifties were exactly the same as they had been for about the last hundred years or so. They were generally known as "London Particulars" and "Pea Soupers" and probably owed a lot to the fact that coal fires were still the normal method of heating everyone`s houses in those days. Central heating was for public buildings and stately homes. David`s interpretation of Richard`s poor health was that it was all my fault of course. I was his mother after all, and it was just not possible that HE, the FATHER and the MAN, could have borne any sort of responsibility for this. Please, ladies, don`t tell me anything about male chauvinist pigs. They have been with us for a very long time indeed, and are not a new invention.

We did have a couple of strokes of good luck in our search for accommodation, however. The first one came when one of my old friends from my Windmill days very kindly offered us the use of her flat as a sort of pied-a-terre. It was near enough to the West End to stop David moaning and was a damn sight more roomy and comfortable than our previous address in the same sort of area. It was also, and most importantly, a lot cheaper! We stayed there for just over a year altogether, after which we were fortunate enough to be offered the chance to take an apartment in a large house in Oxted. Although this was a few miles outside London, it had a socially acceptable address which suited David, and a very nice set of comfortable rooms, making the whole thing completely self-contained which was just up my street. What a nice change not to be constantly bickering about accommodation. The owner and his family were lovely friendly folk who took us into their home and hearts immediately. The bonds we forged then have remained as strong as ever, and Richard and I still keep in touch with them even after all these years.

Quite soon after our arrival I began to work as a sort of au-pair for the lady of the house. It gave me something to do and I had her company for quite a few hours each day, which I thoroughly enjoyed. This "parlourmaid`s position", as he considered it, didn`t suit David one little bit, and he argued and created row after row until I was more or less forced to give it all up. It was shortly after this, in my search for something to stop me turning into a cabbage, that I started to carry on a sort of second-hand relationship with the stage, offering my services for commissions as a choreographer. Quite a lot of work came my way, and I choreographed a fair number of shows, some of them quite important ones. As my confidence grew and my reputation began to be spread by word of mouth, I extended my sphere of operations until I was working on quite a variety of shows and venues, not just in London, but extending over a wide area of the Home Counties.

Not very long after we had arrived, settled down with the family and really begun to enjoy our rural surroundings, a quite well-known horseman who lived nearby offered me a ride - on one of his horses I hasten to add! Amazingly enough, perhaps after the Weymouth/Exmoor fiasco, I still retained a keen interest in horses and riding, so I conditionally accepted his kind offer. As I wasn`t really a free agent, I thought it would be wise to seek David`s approval, even for such a minor item, so I asked him outright. His reply reflecting his loving and caring nature was "Go, and I hope you break your bloody neck!" With these tender endearments firmly in mind, I went off for my ride and nearly DID break my bloody neck as it happened. My mount was very docile indeed, and ambled along very pleasantly until he pricked up his ears as he seemed to recognise a familiar route. Very foolishly I let him have his head and he promptly took off like a rocket, trying to dislodge me by galloping under overhanging branches. I clung on for dear life, even when he started to behave like a bucking bronco. As soon as I could though, I let go and slid to the ground, keeping firm hold of the reins. The loss of his rider had a marvellous calming effect on both the horse and myself, and I led him back to the stables just like a little lamb. The remark on our arrival was, "Oh, you ARE back early." I was much too ashamed to explain the reason for curtailing the ride.

It was quite soon after this little episode that David decided it would be a good idea to obtain a pony for Richard, so that he could learn horsemanship. Although aware that this was probably more to do with David`s social pretension rather than for Richard`s benefit, I had to agree that this was really a sound idea, and would certainly do more good than harm. The foal, a filly, arrived by train at Oxted station, and we were all quite thrilled by her. We housed her in a small field near the house, and David and I took turns through many hours' lungeing and training the animal, who was a very docile, intelligent beast, taking to harness and following our commands very obediently. The term "lungeing" may sound very technical, but all it means is fitting a horse or pony with a head halter and encouraging it to walk, trot and canter around in a circle at the end of a length of rope. This training continues until the animal will obey commands and move at the speed one requires of it. Just to be on the safe side, however, we didn`t rush things, either for the pony or for Richard, and it was about two years before we decided it was completely safe to trust him to try to ride. Richard took to the whole idea immediately, just like a duck to water, and was obviously going to become an accomplished young horseman in a very short time, so we had few qualms about letting him go off on the pony. He called her Cackles and frequently made himself and his mount very useful by riding off into the nearby villages on errands, still on a leading rein with either David or me in charge. We fitted Cackles with a set of pannier baskets, and Cackles would collect, carry and deliver the week`s shopping perfectly happily. The local shopkeepers and their customers thoroughly spoiled Cackles with little treats like carrots and sugar lumps.

With my luck, even this rural idyll couldn`t last. There had to be a snag somewhere. Although the house and its surroundings left little or nothing to be desired, a drawback of the Oxted area was that it tended to be rather damp. After we`d been living there for some time, Richard began to show signs of a return to his old asthmatic condition. At the same time and succeeding in making matters worse, David`s meanness had begun to reassert itself, and he reverted to his former habit of doling out the housekeeping in very small amounts, almost making me beg for each couple of pounds. Naturally, I had to make sure that Richard was properly fed so our financial straits dictated that somebody had to go short. No prizes for guessing who that turned out to be! As a result my own health started to deteriorate quite severely. We were very friendly with our host family who occupied the rest of the house. Because of this, they were quite well aware of our financial, dietary and health problems which they`d obviously discussed amongst themselves. A result of this I`m certain was that the head of the household (whom we`ll call Mr. Smith), offered me a part-time job helping out in a small antique shop he owned in a nearby village. This was only a subsidiary interest for him, in fact, as he was also a successful solicitor with a busy practice. I was reasonably interested and fairly well clued-up about antiques, as well as being in need of the cash, so I accepted the offer gratefully. He was a most generous and kind man, and I`m sure his offer was initially made in good faith. It wasn`t long however, before I noticed him making sheep`s eyes at me, and contriving to get me on my own whenever he could. I`m quite certain that this attraction on his part grew in intensity only after I`d started working at the shop, and wasn`t his prime motive for having offered me the job in the first place. It became obvious that he showed what I can only describe as withdrawal symptoms when my job came to an end and I left the shop. The whole scenario ended up by getting a bit too much for me, because my marriage was going through a sticky patch at the time and an 'en famille' love affair was just the sort of complication I could happily do without. Two further factors affected my thinking. If we`d had an affair, what sort of effect would it have had on his wife and children? Adultery and betrayal under one`s own roof is rather hard to forgive. Also the fact that, although he was a lovely man in so many ways, I just didn`t feel that sort of attraction for him. I was very glad that I`d not tasted the forbidden fruit, when he died very suddenly in his mid-fifties. His loss totally devastated his family, and I felt so sad for them.

On the occasions when he could be prised away from his pony, Richard`s main playmate was Judith, grand daughter of Mr. and Mrs. Smith and the apple of their eyes. They got on well together and I can`t remember them ever quarrelling over anything. They used to wander freely around the house and garden, and I recall one very memorable occasion when they fancied some pretty berries which grew on a bush at the bottom of the garden. Judith ate quite a few of them, and it was only by great good fortune that I happened to go down into the garden and saw what was going on. I immediately called Pat, Judith`s mother, who showed far more presence of mind than I had. She got Judith into the house and gave her lots of salt water to drink, with the inevitable result. This quick action on her part could well have saved her daughter`s life, because we never found out exactly what the berries were.

In addition to his chronic meanness, David had another loveable characteristic. A rather nasty cruel streak which manifested itself in words rather than physical abuse. He probably felt frustrated and bitter over something or other, just like we all do on occasion, but then he would take out his spite on Richard and myself. There was never any question of our sitting down together and talking about any of his, or our troubles. He just wasn`t that sort of man. This behaviour of his was a little extra which, added to my already inadequate diet and continuous worries about money, succeeded in turning me into a rather sick woman. Mr. and Mrs. Smith noticed this. How could they miss it? They became concerned to the extent that they arranged for me to see their own family doctor. This was in the early days of the NHS, when surgeries were jam-packed with people getting teeth and glasses they didn`t need, just because they were free. In order to bypass what could have been a long wait, Mr. and Mrs. Smith insisted I should see the doctor as a private patient. The family paid all the dues, something for which I have always been grateful. The doctor spent quite a lot of time examining me. More than I could have expected if I`d been an NHS patient I suppose. He asked a lot of questions obviously noticing that I was not as well as I should have been and looked far older than my years. His advice was quite clear. "Ditch that so-and-so of a husband of yours and get yourself some sort of a life for yourself and your child just as quickly as you can!" The more I thought about it, the more I realised that the doctor`s advice was sound and should be followed. Richard and I packed our bags and decamped very soon afterwards, moving to Pinner to stay with the mother of another of my friends, who was again called Pat. She happily agreed to take care of Richard, leaving me free to look for stage work, or whatever else I could get.

CHAPTER FOURTEEN

Back Into Showbiz

The first reasonable job that came along was in the laboratory of Bencards, a firm on the Great West Road, not too far away. This left my evenings free for other activities and I lost no time in joining the Alex Charles Concert Party. This was a small company made up of true enthusiasts, and we played at venues throughout the London area. As well as my own direct part in the party, I was also carrying out choreographic commissions, mainly for a company of eight dancers, who toured with another small company, offering a range of cabaret items.

Alex Charles London Cabaret with magic

An important fringe benefit which came my way as a result of this work was that I met the fabulous Louise Browne, who was then a Director of the Royal Ballet. Louise very graciously asked me to help her with her own ballet school which was located nearby. Needless to say I didn`t wait to be asked twice! Louise was a tremendously talented performer in her own right, having pursued a glittering career in her native USA for many years before coming over here. She and I co-operated on a number of productions and worked together in several plays. My own favourite was "The Scarlet Pimpernel," in which I played Suzanne de Tournai to Louise`s Lady Blakeney. They really were such happy and wonderful times. What a pity they had to end. They did end however, and in a rather unexpected way. The many venues where we played included several of the London parks, where we performed in the open air, usually attracting quite large and appreciative audiences. Quite a few months had passed since my split up with David and there had been no communication of any sort between us in the meantime. This didn`t bother me in the slightest, as Richard and I were both surviving particularly well. There was always enough to eat and perhaps more importantly peace at home.

I had a couple of dancing spots in the show and had just finished one of them and gone backstage. I was in time to overhear one of the girls talking about a city gent she had spotted in the audience. This chap, so she said, had the full uniform of black suit, bowler hat and umbrella and stuck out like a sore thumb among the casually dressed strollers who made up our usual type of audience. No prizes for guessing who this city gent turned out to be! He came backstage after the show, congratulated me on my performance, presented me with a bouquet of flowers - the full works. He told me that he`d actually employed a private detective to find me, as he found very soon after our bust up that he couldn`t live without Richard and me. He begged me to forgive him and come back, everything would be different, he`d seen the error of his ways, etc. etc. The scene has doubtless been repeated throughout history, one way or another, and I expect reconciliations have actually worked on some occasions. Ours didn`t, as it happened, but it took a while for me to find that out. Anyway, at the time I thought it might be worth another go, so as soon as my contract with the concert party terminated, my son and I went back to David.

David still nursed strong ambitions to return to what he called his "roots" back down in Wales. My own experiences of that land were very happy ones. Memories of the lovely times I`d spent during my service with the ATS at Manorbier were still quite fresh, so I had no qualms about moving back to live there. Off we went house hunting, because David considered that we could make a very good living from farming. During this search we stayed in a small friendly hotel in Carmarthen and did the rounds of all the local estate agents, auctioneers, and solicitors as we looked at many properties over a wide area of Carmarthenshire and Cardiganshire. Unlike anglicised South Pembrokeshire this was the true heartland where quite a high percentage of people spoke Welsh. They also used English as well, so I had no fears about being able to communicate. David himself already spoke the language quite fluently and I expected, quite correctly as it turned out, that Richard would also be able to pick it up easily.

Many, many years after all these happenings, I started to learn Welsh myself, with a satisfying degree of success, even if I say so myself. Then as now, people who were trying to sell properties used a language all of their own, and we soon learned to avoid anything which was described as `improvable` or `with full scope for modernisation` as they were invariably ramshackle, and sometimes total ruins. They usually smelled of damp and decay and I swear that if we`d kept quiet enough we`d have been able to hear the woodworm munching away in the roofs.

CHAPTER FIFTEEN

Our West Wales Mansion - Alltyrodyn

At long, long last after what seemed like thousands of totally unsuitable places, there came a turn for the better. We were offered a lovely sounding property called Alltyrodyn Mansion, or more correctly by its Welsh title Plas Alltyrodyn. It was part of a quite large and important estate, running to some 475 acres in total, and mostly made up of good pasture and arable land. Alltyrodyn actually means "Hill of the Lime Kiln" but we never found the kiln, or any other evidence of lime burning in the area. The land in fact didn`t seem to be deficient in lime, or anything else for that matter. By a strange sort of coincidence, David already knew the property from having attended parties there. It had previously been owned by his friend Dougie Stewart, who had been a confirmed party host for many years. I fell in love with the place at first sight. The house itself was a beautiful properly-proportioned Georgian mansion, a little down at heel and neglected of course, but then it had been empty for the past three years or so and the survey which we commissioned showed that there was nothing seriously wrong with the buildings generally. A bit of spit and polish and some loving care would cure everything I was certain. David was also very enthusiastic which made me feel perhaps just a shade too optimistically that this was a place where we could all pull together, to a common purpose and really be happy.

One of the first effects of our move from town to country was that it brought the transport problem into sharp focus. We`d been thoroughly spoiled in London and the Home Counties where there were buses, trains, the Tube and for very special occasions as far as we were concerned, taxis. Out here there was NOTHING, apart from shanks`s pony, a horse and cart, or perhaps a bicycle. Car ownership was nothing near as widespread as it is today, even in the affluent city and suburban areas, and country folk didn`t normally have that sort of money anyway. David had actually visited the Motor Show in 1925, and had bought there and then, a brand new Talbot 25 H.P. saloon. Just to prove if proof were needed how miserly he was, he still had the damn thing, after all these years. Incredible isn`t it? It was obviously well past its sell-by date, but there was no sign of David ever parting with this pride and joy of his, so we had to grin and bear it, trying not to wince as it banged and bounced us through even the shallowest of potholes.

Alltyrodyn, Llandyssul

There was no form of heating, so we had to wrap ourselves up like Eskimos for even the shortest journey in winter. It was quite frustrating sitting there shivering and seeing clouds of steam puffing out of the radiator and going to waste. Just a note in passing even if we`d bought a brand new car in the early 1950`s it might not even then have had a heater fitted. Heaters were EXTRA and cost quite a bit over the odds. At that time, they weren`t even particularly reliable, so there was a fair chance of cold journeys anyway.

We duly completed the mountains of paperwork, signed our names on dozens of dotted lines and agreed to part with what seemed like a King`s ransom each month in the way of mortgage payments. We had already visualised the difficulties of keeping up such a large house with its attendant grounds, especially in view of its rather neglected condition. The only practical solution it seemed would be to buy the adjoining semi-derelict farm property, which was also part of the estate. We could then run this as a practical farm to earn the wherewithal, running a milking herd and growing a wide range of crops. Potatoes, kale and turnips were all items which would grow very well in this area, but it all meant a lot of hard work. David airily dismissed any possibility of financial problems. We had got ourselves a prime chunk of farming land, and we were jolly well going to work it to return us a substantial profit. Nothing for it then but to put on one`s best pair of rose-tinted glasses and have a go. So that`s exactly what we did.

On our arrival to take up residence at Plas Alltyrodyn, we turned into the rather neglected driveway, passing a pair of quite ornate wrought iron gates, which hung from stone pillars at the entrance. Our elderly jalopy bumped and shuddered along the surface and I made a mental note that we would have to get some sort of repairs done very soon. That was one of the tremendous number of jobs, large and small, which would occupy us for the next eighteen years, which was the total time we spent at the house. When we pulled up in front of the house, I looked up at it and gave a huge sigh - it was the strangest feeling - I felt just as if I was coming back home, although I`d hardly had a really good look at the place up until then. I turned to David excitedly and exclaimed "This is our home and it`s beautiful and I`m going to call it my white elephant, because it`s NEARLY white and it seems that nobody but us has wanted it for ever such a long time. It`s been standing here empty, just waiting for us, for over three years!" David laughed. "In that case, I`d better carry you over the threshold." He tried his best to do so, but had to put me down in quite a hurry. This was NOT because I had put on weight, I hasten to point out, but solely due to the old shrapnel wound which David sustained during the Great War, and which had torn some of the muscles and tendons in his right arm and leg.

The house and the many things that happened there, played a very important part in the lives of all three of us, so perhaps a detailed description would be relevant. It wasn`t of course a stately home in the normal sense of the term, but it was big and imposing, and had many features of interest. Also as I`ve already admitted I was totally in love with the place from the very beginning. On either side of the drive grew enormous clumps of rhododendrons, interspersed with a few prime beeches. We arrived at precisely the right time of year to see the swathes of daffodils in all their finery. Quite a sight! After passing the rhododendrons the vista opened out and one could see, over on the right, some of the fields belonging to the adjoining farm, which now belonged to us. The land rose to form a hill, on top of which was an earthwork which had formerly been the site of an ancient motte and bailey castle, probably dating from the early Iron Age. This fortification was known as Castell Hywel (Hywel`s Castle, or Howell`s castle, depending on whether you spell his name in Welsh or English). It was reputed to have been the site of a fierce battle at some time in the 12th century. Funny how history repeats itself. The house and grounds were also to be battle sites in the 20th century, seeing daggers drawn by me and my darling spouse.

As one continued along the drive, the next feature of interest was and still is, the Cold Bath. It was one of those features which it`s not possible to date with any accuracy, but informed guesswork puts it as being installed in the late sixteenth or early seventeenth centuries, when it is known that a lot of refurbishment work went on, and when bathing requirements were quite a bit more spartan than they are today. The bath was constructed in stonework in the form of a sort of trough about nine feet square, with a set of steps leading down into the water. A stone gargoyle fed the bath, spouting spring water from its mouth. In all the years we lived at Alltyrodyn, which included some pretty dry summers, I never remember that spring ever drying up, although its flow did diminish in quantity on a couple of occasions. On one of the walls which surrounded the bath was installed a line of wooden clothes hooks. The purpose of the bath, as I was later told by locals who knew the place and whose forebears had worked on the estate or in the house for generations, was to enable the men to strip off and take a cooling dip after a day`s hunting. To me, this was a horrible thought as the water was always ice cold and there was no possible means of heating it. After passing the Bath, another hundred and fifty yards travel brought one to a point where the house came quite suddenly into view. The house was always very light in colour and in fact, tended to look a bit stark against its lush green backdrop of beech, maple and oak, with rhododendrons and azaleas adding their own special splashes of colour in season. As already noted, the house had stood empty and rather neglected for over three years until we came along, with only occasional visits from the estate agent to check for damage. We found that quite a few other people had also visited the place, but they were only interested in nosing around and looking at its glories and not concerned enough (or perhaps daft enough) to buy it. In front of the house, the drive opened up to form a wide turning circle, in the centre of which was a pond complete with ornamental fountain. On the side of the circle farthest from the house, a flight of stone steps led down to a field, which featured a haha, or sunken fence. Years later, when we had to call in plumbers to carry out repairs, they had to explore the field and surrounding area to find out exactly where the pipework was running. Quite close to the haha they discovered a small door which led to a passageway about four feet high. At my request, they went in to have a look around, and reported that they`d found quite a maze of passageways under the drive, and also a small, but stout, padlocked door. I`ve kicked myself mentally about this ever since, because I should have told them then and there to break down the door and find out what lay beyond it. We`d have been quite happy to employ the plumbers to do the deed, because neither David nor I ever had the slightest inclination to go nosing around in there for ourselves, for reasons which will shortly become apparent. Beyond the turning circle and covering the whole area between the main drive and the less important South drive, was a large lawn, which we eventually managed to rescue, to the extent that we were able to play tennis there a few years later. At the end of the lawn farthest from the house was a small Memorial Garden dedicated to the memory of Lieutenant Alex Stuart who had lived there and who had been killed in the Great War. The garden had obviously been someone`s labour of love. It was surrounded by low walls, with archways here and there, and a few stone urns. It was the sort of place, which it`s impossible not to respect, and I later tried to embellish the garden with some flowers and shrubs. In spite of my best efforts, however, I never succeeded in getting anything to grow there at all. From the side of the tennis lawn, a set of stone steps led up to a pretty walk flanked by azaleas, and ending at a black and white octagonal summerhouse. This little hideaway was furnished with wooden seats fixed around the walls and the windows were glazed with quite ornate stained glass panels, which had been removed from the village church in nearby Capel Dewi, following its renovation some years ago.

Tennis lawn, at the side of Alltyrodyn

Returning to the front of the main house and looking towards one`s left, one would see another field in which the outline of a Roman Fort could just be made out. The fort had never been excavated or disturbed in any way, but its outline became quite clear after any prolonged spell of dry weather. The then curator of the county museum in Carmarthen professed a keen interest in the site, as there was apparently a large amount of documentation about the Fort already deposited in the Museum. It was one of his intentions to have a series of aerial photographs taken, prior to setting up an excavation project, but he never got around to doing anything about it. I was a bit disappointed about this, both at the time and during the intervening years. How exciting it might have been, and what treasures we might have unearthed. Still, no good crying about spilt milk.

The Alltyrodyn estate was full of many sources of interest. The house itself was totally fascinating and HAUNTED!! Hence our reluctance to go poking about in underground passages. There had, it appears, been a building on the site as far back as the 13th century but nobody seemed to know exactly what sort of building it was. Some three hundred years later a fairly substantial manor house was built here for the convenience of the first High Sheriff of the County of Cardigan, whose name we were never interested enough to find out, and he lived there for quite a few years. During the seventeenth and eighteenth centuries some substantial alterations and improvements were made to various parts of the structure and its environs including the construction of a completely new facade to the main house and the building of a stable block, carriage house and granary.

Mixed with my enthrallment at the house and the prospects of living there, my rose-coloured glasses did tend to slip now and again, and I began to be just a little bit apprehensive about how we`d cope with the upkeep and management of such a huge place. Up until then, David, Richard and I had lived together in the small terraced house which we shared with my parents and a selection of flats and apartments. This house had fourteen bedrooms, including the servants' quarters; eighteen acres of garden and 475 acres of agricultural holding which was located on the other side of the valley, necessitating quite a fair round trip for every visit. David however, was far from sharing any of my fears, was in his element, or in his oils as the local idiom put it. He assured me with all the aplomb of the country squire and gentleman farmer, that all would be well, nothing could possibly go wrong, and we would do famously.

Inside the house, we came first to the entrance hallway. This was set out in a design closely resembling that of the Designer/Architect Adam. There was an enormous fireplace, which had a very ornate, carved oak surround and we understood that it had been taken from another Welsh mansion - we never found out which one - and had been brought to the house quite a long time ago. This fireplace dated from the seventeenth century and although was quite out of place in the opinion of some purists, was a thing of great beauty in its own right. Off the hall to the left, was a room which later became our dining room, whilst the corresponding room on the right had a fine moulded ceiling with a design of vine leaves and grapes. It was also notable for a large ornate floor to ceiling mirror and an Adam fireplace. A genuine one this time. From the entrance hallway, a set of double doors led through to an inner hall, sporting a set of full-height Georgian mirrors around the walls, and with a centrepiece made up of a wonderful Regency marble topped table in a black and gilt finish. From this hallway a magnificent staircase led to the upper storeys. The treads and risers were of native oak, flanked by mahogany banisters. Truly a sight to behold! Lighting the first turning of the staircase was a nine foot high stained glass window incorporating the arms of the Stewart family, owners of the house and estate from about 1820 until the mid-1940s.

Retracing our steps down to the ground floor and looking around the inner hall we become aware of the other doors giving access to a couple of further rooms. The first of these was a narrow, uninteresting and rather gloomy room, which we decided was better kept to ourselves. It became our office, and we were quite happy to close the door on it at the end of the day, leaving our books and pens until the next day. Next door, couldn`t have been more of a contrast. This was by far the most beautiful room in the whole house. It had a polished oak floor, regency alcoves and lighting sconces. Two huge Georgian windows let in plenty of light and afforded a panoramic view across the lawn and the Memorial Garden. A fine ornately carved walnut fireplace was a major feature of the room, and we learned from one of our neighbours that this was in fact a genuine and rather rare Adam, which had again been removed from another mansion and brought here. It`s quite possible that this lovely room could have been used as a ballroom in bygone days. It was certainly large and imposing enough. That lovely floor was absolutely ideal for dancing. Sometimes I would stand in the doorway and let my imagination run away with me, picturing the room full of fine ladies and their escorts all dressed in the high fashion of the time in satins and silks, with powdered wigs and whirling around the place to the music of a small orchestra. We did get as close as we could to this ideal, making this our own music room. David forgot his mean streak to the extent of buying me a lovely Broadwood grand piano some years later. This made an ideal centrepiece for the room and we eventually held all sorts of soirees and a few Hunt Balls, which everybody seemed to enjoy very much.

On the other side of the hallway a long dark passage led to the business centre of the house. This comprised the butler`s pantry, the housekeeper`s room and the kitchen. Along one wall of the passage up near ceiling level hung a series of wire operated bells hanging from springs. These were used to summon servants to various parts of the house. Under a trapdoor in the floor, a cavity of about five feet square and four feet high housed the ancient and none too reliable central heating boiler, which was of course, coal fired. We learned that a maid servant had been very badly burned in an incident some years previously when the boiler blew back. I expect that in accordance with the custom at that time, the family shrugged its collective shoulders and simply replaced the poor girl without a second thought. Or am I being a bit uncharitable? I don`t suppose we`ll ever know.

As befitted a Manor House, the kitchen was truly enormous, with what must have been about a hundred hooks screwed into the ceiling. It wasn`t too difficult to imagine them holding game, fowl, sides of bacon and the like, during the "Good Old Days." A scrubbed table, easily big enough to seat twenty people, stood in the centre of the room. There were occasions later on when I actually catered for that number of casual farmworkers, having to do all the cooking for them on my own. This happened during a period when we had to engage quite a few extra pairs of hands to help out with an intensive tree planting programme which we undertook at the time. A flight of steep and not very well lit steps led down from the kitchen, giving access to a sizeable complex of cellars. These held many yards of wooden racking and some of the "bins" contained a variety of elderly bottles. Many of the labels bore dates running well back into the last century, making the bottles themselves museum pieces in their own right. Over time, I got around to blowing the dust off most of them, eagerly scanning each label just in case a genuine Napoleon brandy or true vintage wine would come to light, but no, somebody had got there first and I was unlucky again.

My visit to the cellars did however, prompt a new idea, which I was certain would make our fortune with minimum effort. We would grow MUSHROOMS! They are always in demand and, even then, commanded premium prices for good quality produce. Just a little later on, almost as soon as we considered ourselves established in the house, we cleared away a lot of the racking and installed tables all as recommended in the books we read on the subject. Then we carried loads and loads of fresh and potent farmyard manure and a huge quantity of straw into the cellar and spread it over the tables. Finally we bought the appropriate recommended mushroom spawn, sowed it with care and tended it as lovingly as we knew how. Alas, it all went totally haywire and all we had to show for our efforts was a very smelly cellar, a lot of dirt to clean up and about half a pound of yucky maggot infested fungi. It took a long time to get everything back as it had been, but at least we had learned another salutary lesson.

Going back upstairs again and into the main kitchen, a door led into what would nowadays be called the utility room. At Alltyrodyn it was known as "Y Gegin Fach." Literally, the Little Kitchen. This housed the enormous general purpose sink, made of stoneware and of a pattern known as a Belfast Sink. It would have been possible easily for a petite adult and certainly for a child to have taken a bath in it. Above the sink a pair of brass taps fed hot and cold water. When these were turned on fully, the amount of water they gushed would have satisfied the local fire brigade quite happily. It was certainly the best possible method of washing large quantities of vegetables before peeling them. Beyond the little kitchen, another doorway led into a smaller room, fitted with a couple of stone slabs and two shallow sinks, again with hot and cold water supplied by large brass taps. This was the "Abattoir" of the house, where the pigs were brought to be "dealt with" and converted into a vast array of eatables. "Cured" is perhaps a very inappropriate word to describe the treatment meted out to the poor unfortunate porkers in this room, but it`s an ideal example of the peculiarities with which the English language is riddled. From the curing room a further narrow corridor led into what had previously been used as the servants' hall. This had fallen into disuse for many years, and remained rather neglected until we cleaned it up a few years later on and turned it into a sort of convalescent home for our quite large collection of sick animals and birds. Very soon after our arrival at the house I realised, or became aware of my deep love for all kinds of animals and creatures. Having been a real "townie" for most of my previous life, pets and so forth took second place to my other interests of dance and boyfriends! Now, it was going to be possible for me to live with Nature on hopefully amicable and rewarding terms. Another part of my education which took place a few years later on was that our then housekeeper, Mrs. W., taught me the mysteries of salting and curing the meat for myself. I was never happy about the whole process and couldn`t possibly bring myself to eat the resulting bacon, especially after it had been hanging for months from the kitchen ceiling hooks. My husband however, `bless him` thought the resulting home cured product quite delicious and devoured it with relish. It was a parallel with his habit of eating game and similar flesh when it was, to me at any rate, almost rancid and only fit for the dustbin. Pheasant, hare and so on was always kept far longer than it should have been, even if one followed custom and practice, and venison when we could get hold of any was buried and not dug up for consumption until several months later. There`s just no accounting for some people`s tastes, and one of life`s greatest mysteries to me is exactly how David managed to avoid food poisoning. He must have had a cast iron digestion.

Leaving the main kitchen through yet another door, we enter the courtyard. This was partly roofed over by a verandah, and a suite of four rooms led off it. Three of the rooms were used for storage of various items. Unfortunately we never found anything of real value in any of them. The fourth was the estate laundry. In here stood an enormous brick built structure, with a space underneath it to accommodate a fire. The brickwork surrounded a copper boiler, some five feet in diameter, and dating back Goodness knows how far. This was the place where all the household linen had been washed for quite a few generations. Needless to say it wasn`t too long before this bit of apparatus was replaced by a rather more up to date washing machine. A door set into the rear wall of the courtyard led to the bell tower, which still contained the original bell. This could be used and in fact was used by us on several occasions to summon anyone working on the farm or in the fields, if they were urgently required. The bell tower was also the well-established home of a pair of barn owls, who never seemed particularly bothered by us, even on the occasions when we had to ring the bell.

If we go back from the courtyard into the kitchen, we find a set of stairs, nothing like as grand as the main staircase in the hall. This sort of secondary flight led up to a very neglected set of rooms set directly over the kitchen and probably part of the servant`s quarters, together with two fully fitted bathrooms and a lavatory. The fittings belonged to a bygone age and these had deteriorated until they were completely unusable. An awful lot of the fixtures and fittings in the house would have been far more at home in a museum in fact. In addition to the "suite" mentioned, a door at the top of this flight of stairs led into the Brown Room. This room had a chequered history to say the least. Some years after we`d moved in and settled down we had a visit from Lady Bruce, former wife of Dougie Stewart, who at the time was living in Ireland. In the course of conversation, she asked us if we ever used the Brown Room. "I tried it for a while and I had to move out" she said. "There was always an air of something evil there. Horrible faces used to appear at the window, although the room is on the first floor." This remark caused me quite a bit of disquiet, because we ourselves had experienced something "not quite right" about the place on a number of occasions. In one instance a visitor from Germany had stayed there. Although she didn`t say anything at all during her stay with us, we found a note which she had left for us. It read through obviously in German, "Beware of the ghost!!"

To one side of the Brown Room a short passageway led into the main first floor corridor, linking up with the head of the main staircase, which had doors leading into two of the bedrooms and two of the associated dressing rooms as well. There was also a pair of "Powder Closets" set between the dressing rooms and the bedrooms, which we pressed into service as fitted wardrobes. This suite of rooms was set in the front of the house, commanding breathtaking panoramic views across and down the valley in the general direction of Capel Dewi village. A further very large bedroom overlooking the tennis lawn and fitted up with ensuite bathroom just a shade more up to date than those already mentioned completed the accommodation on the first floor. A continuation of the secondary stairs led on and up to the second floor, where a set of eight rooms made up the servants sleeping quarters and bathroom. With just this one way up and down, it`s not difficult to speculate what would have happened in case of fire. There was no possibility of escape from this top storey. A reminder, perhaps, just like the incident where the servant was badly burned with the downblast from the central heating boiler, that servants lives were of little value and domestics easily replaced.

CHAPTER SIXTEEN

Hauntings

The local folk told us with great relish all the tales of the ghosts of Alltyrodyn. And some of the stories were pretty lurid to say the least. A spectral carriage and four was said to travel the main drive quite often and had been seen by many people over the years. I resisted the temptation to ask if these sightings occurred on the way to the pub or on the way home!! A young girl had been seen combing her hair in front of the fireplace in the Red Room, and everybody seemed to know about the faces which appeared in the window of the Brown Room exactly as Lady Bruce had described. Although I don`t count myself as superstitious or easily frightened, I made sure I chose the Green Room for our own sleeping quarters, with Richard occupying the adjoining Green Dressing Room. No point tempting providence. There must have been some point and substance to at least some of the `haunting' tales, because we ourselves experienced some odd happenings during our time at the house. These included manifestations and mysterious sounds. The first indication as far as I recall was on an occasion when my sister-in-law was staying with us, and saw the figure of a lady, dressed in the fashion of a century ago glide noiselessly from a point underneath the main staircase and cross the inner hall, to disappear through one of the mirrors. After that experience she flatly refused to remain alone in any of the rooms in the house. Somebody had to be there on every occasion, even to the extent of standing outside the "loo" when she was in occupation there!

On another occasion, David and I were entertaining eight guests. We had just sat down to dinner when we heard heavy footsteps approaching the dining room door.

I emphasise that all ten of us heard the same thing. David rose from his chair, saying "That must be White" who was one of the farm hands. "Perhaps something has gone wrong at the farm. Excuse me please I shan`t be a moment." I jumped up as well as I was seated nearest to the door, and opened it. There was nobody there. On thinking things through we realised that nobody could have come in from outside anyway, because we`d secured all the outer doors.

The son of one of our guests was put into the Brown Room to sleep. In the middle of the night we heard him call out in fear. Something had touched his face and awakened him and he was certain that there was someone standing beside his bed. I had to make up another bed for him in his parents room as he flatly refused to stay in the room, insisting on spending the rest of the night close to Mum and Dad. Some little time after this we put Richard to sleep in the Brown Room just for one night. I think there was some decorating work going on affecting his normal sleeping arrangements. Anyway he too woke in the middle of the night screaming "Mummy, Mummy, I`m frightened." Obviously we hadn`t mentioned the incident of the other little boy to Richard, so he couldn`t possibly have been affected by that happening. I dashed in to see what was wrong, and found him shaking with fear and quite inconsolable. I had to get into bed with him. Eventually he calmed down enough for us both to drop off to sleep, but even this bit of peace wasn`t to last long. We were awakened again by the sound of slow, heavy footsteps coming up the secondary staircase from the kitchen. The steps stopped right outside the door of our room. As can be imagined both Richard and I were petrified, clinging to each other for all we were worth. After a short while we heard the steps again. They seemed to be moving along the corridor until they finally stopped again outside the other door of the Brown Room. Perhaps unsurprisingly, neither of us got a great deal of sleep for the remainder of the night.

Another somewhat disturbed night I can remember happened when David was in hospital. He`d sustained a broken collar bone, but the medical staff insisted that he stay overnight, just in case of any complications. We had no living-in staff at that time, and Richard was away as a boarder in prep school, so I was alone apart from Pete, our Boxer dog. Quite apart from the hauntings, the mere fact of being all alone in that huge isolated house was pretty unnerving anyway, so I wasn`t feeling too happy for starters. Without any warning, Pete sat up growling with his hackles up, and his eyes seemed to be following something passing from one end of the room to the other. That was IT I could take no more! I threw a dressing gown over me, called Pete to follow and dashed downstairs and out onto the drive. Oddly enough, once I was out in the fresh air and had taken a couple of deep breaths, I felt much more self-possessed, calmer and safer. Even so, it was quite some time later before I could bring myself to re-enter the house, and I was only able to cat-nap for the rest of the night. It must have been just about the longest night I`ve ever experienced in my entire life. The hearing of footsteps mostly at night became almost commonplace. They were heard in various parts of the house on a variety of occasions, and by different people, sometimes alone, at other times in groups. One of our guests remarked that he`d had a bit of trouble in getting off to sleep because of the noise of someone walking up and down the corridor outside his room. He said it sounded for all the world like somebody in Army boots or heavy working footwear.

We had resigned ourselves to having to put up with these hauntings for the rest of our lives, when they suddenly ceased altogether. Nevertheless, it was quite a long time before we thought it safe to relax, but the passage of time seemed to show that we had nothing to fear. In fact, after the first four years we spent at Alltyrodyn, we were never disturbed ever again. Some considerable time later, I happened to mention the happenings to a clairvoyant of my acquaintance. Her explanation was that as the ghostly happenings went on for four years, which was the same length of time that the Great War had lasted. Could our spectre or at least one of them, have been the restless spirit of Alex Stewart, who we knew had been killed in that war, and who had as it were come back home for a few years? This far from being an explanation posed a question to which I`ve never been able to find a satisfactory answer.

CHAPTER SEVENTEEN

Life With David

Life at Alltyrodyn wasn`t confined to dealing with things that go bump in the night. Neither was it all dinner parties, soirees and resident guests. We had a sizeable mortgage to pay, and our only way of earning the necessary was by the sweat of our brows, through the almost continuous slog of running a mixed farm. Although crops and vegetables needed a lot of backbreaking work to keep them up to scratch, at least they didn`t fight back, as some of the animals seemed to do on occasions. Our cows in particular appeared to take some sort of perverse delight in flicking away at me with their tails, especially when those appendages were liberally covered with fresh, soft and sticky dung. There was one very special occasion which I remember, because it cost us a lot of money. I was in one of the fields, minding my own business, when I got a bit too near one of our cows. She flicked her great mucky tail right across my face, nothing new in that except that this time the blow dislodged one of my micro contact lenses. Out it fell into the grass. Of course, finding it again was a total impossibility, as it was such a tiny object. The last straw came when we realised that we`d forgotten to renew the insurance on the lenses, and that replacement was going to cost the then very substantial sum of fifty pounds. This was something which we could ill afford at the time, but needs must, so we made the best of it. Other facets of country life which we had to adopt were such items as milking by hand and being prepared to saw off part of the horns of a cow to release her from entanglement in a hedge. One night I helped our local vet to perform an emergency Caesarian on one of our herd although, to be honest, my part in the proceedings was mainly threading needles for him. He couldn`t see to do the job himself.

Ladies who want to retain husband, dignity and sanity, though not necessarily in that order must never under any circumstances allow their better halves to teach them to drive. This is especially so if the lessons take place in an elderly tractor on a hill farm. The trauma involved in this setup can be equated with a death in the family, moving house or even a multiple birth. The agricultural part of our estate was a hill farm and, in Wales, hills REALLY are hills! They are certainly not the most suitable of places to learn to manoeuvre a tractor, especially when the machine is past its best and, to say the least, a bit temperamental. I got really badly stuck one day on the side of one of the hills. It was called Y Fron. No it's not the men`s underpants with two letters missing! Literally translated Y Fron means "The Breast" and it usually describes a conical sort of hill, looking a little bit like a breast I suppose, and normally covered with a reasonable amount of grass or other vegetation. A hill of similar shape but devoid of such growth would be called Y Foel, which translates more or less as "Baldy!" Now the Welsh lesson is over, for the time being. Now we`ll return to me, my ever helpful husband and the tractor. All I could do was to hang on to the machine, which was tilted at a quite dangerous angle, and scream for help. "I can`t get the B****y thing into gear, what can I do?" I shouted at the top of my lungs. My husband`s reply reflected his obvious concern for my safety and well-being. "You'll have to figure it out for yourself you silly bitch." We ranted and raved away at each other full blast for quite a long time, our raised voices echoing and carrying quite clearly across the valley. In the village, where doubtless every word could be heard, lived the God-fearing chapel goers who never themselves swore or did anything of much consequence at all, or they didn`t do so where they could be heard or seen. I`m quite sure we must have completed their education in the finer points of Anglo Saxon, both at that time and on other similar occasions whilst we happily farmed away among them. I spent many hours slaving away on that tractor, and gradually became quite expert in handling it. Over the years it developed quite a number of idiosyncrasies and lovable habits, like fading or completely failing brakes and erratic steering. One day, I was driving it full bore up quite a steep hill, having made the fundamental error of having put it into too high a gear. The inevitable happened. It stalled. As soon as I shoved the clutch down and put it into neutral, the beast started to run away backwards down the hill gathering speed as it went. I stamped on the brake pedal and pulled up the handbrake all to no avail. Trying hard not to panic and jump for it, I steered the tractor towards the roadside bank, which at that point was made up of comparatively soft earth and grass. I was lucky, although the damn thing rocked and rolled all over the place, the speed gradually bled away until I was able to jam it securely into the banking. A shivering jelly stepped down from the driving seat, to receive a monumental row from David. "That was a damn silly thing to do. You know it hasn`t got any brakes!" If I HAD known did he think I`d have been stupid enough to have tried driving it at all?

Another potential `powder keg` which dogged me at various times during the years we spent at Alltyrodyn was that I had an unfortunate habit of attracting the attention of men! I never did anything to encourage them. We had numerous or perhaps more correctly, innumerable visits from the various males of the species in all shapes and sizes and all of them married. I could not understand why they needed to stray, unless it was the fact that I had married a man who was 24 years older than me, and old enough to be my father. Were they just sorry for me? I don`t think so! Among the bevy of men was a wealthy company director with his South American wife. They appeared to be happy together, and I got to like them both, but who is to know what their lives were like behind closed doors? Then there was the scrap iron dealer who called several times. He became very intense, so much so that I was so scared I had to contact the local police, because I was concerned about my safety. He wanted me to run away with him, but he also threatened my life, if I did not. Then there was a local farmer who used to drive me to the operatic group. We used to perform with this group, because we were both singers. He had a particularly fine tenor voice, but again he became over-fond. He had a lovely wife and he was father to eight children. A local plumber who had a lot of work on hand at Alltyrodyn tried to rape me. My doctor also tried it on, thinking I needed some comfort, when my husband and I were going through a difficult time. I told him a definite "no" but at the same time he had been a wonderful kind person who had understood our situation, and offered help. I never reported him to the medical authorities as I think he had misunderstood what I needed. The last man was a director of social services. When my husband threw me out because I could not perform my wifely duties, owing to his intense cruelty, this man arranged to put me up in a flat in Carmarthen. Eventually he left his wife and bought a flat which we shared very happily for many years. I never had an affair with any of them except of course the last one. Having had such a horrendous birth when my son was born I never wanted to go through that again and that kept me on the 'straight and narrow'. No man ever came near me. Pregnancy was a 'no' word. My efforts to remain pure, were not helped by the fact that my marriage was in so many ways more hellish than "made in heaven."

However, stick it out is what I did, so nobody could ever have pointed an accusing finger at me for anything in that context. I was fully aware of the mortal danger of giving David any sort of ammunition to use against me. As things turned out in the end, it might all have ended up in precisely the same sort of way if I had said "To Hell with it" at the time, embarked on a fling or two, or even a series of more serious affairs, and maybe have been able to enjoy just a little bit of happiness. Oh, for a crystal ball! Even though he had to work very hard for long hours, and ended up with a lot of dirt under his fingernails, the purchase of Alltyrodyn and its environs caused a total resurgence of David`s snobbery. He referred to the majority of people, especially the locals and our neighbours as "The Common Herd," and I was actively discouraged from any sort of familiarity with them. "They`re really only peasantry after all." I should henceforth he said, seek to mix only with those people who could be considered high born and of a better class, - even if they were destitute! Pedigree and breeding were, if anything, more important for people than for cattle, and Lady Trowbridge`s Book of Etiquette was taken out, dusted off and thrust under my nose again, with an instruction from David to re-read it and follow its precepts.

The various visitors to our house obviously included my parents who came down from London on a number of occasions over the years. Although I was glad to see them especially as they enjoyed pretty good health, I was always just a bit nervous whenever they were with us. I realised that any little faux pas or social gaffe on the part of Mother or Dad would be picked up by David and dissected and cruelly criticised after they had departed. "I knew I`d made a mistake marrying into a family that doesn`t even know one type of knife from another," would be a typical put-down. As if it mattered anyway! As a result I invited my parents less and less frequently, preferring to go up to London and visit them, away from David and his nit-picking. By this time Mother had totally recovered and it was difficult to imagine just how desperately ill she had been. She lived to the ripe old age of eighty two, dying very suddenly and without too much pain. Dad was lost without her for a while, but decided it was no good to mope around doing nothing. He himself was eighty one and for the best part of a lifetime had been looked after by Mother and me. Nothing daunted, he took over the cooking as though it was second nature to him. His specialities were bread pudding, stews and hot pots which were truly delicious. I loved them! Dad carried on his solitary life for a further twelve years, keeping reasonably active and in full possession of his faculties until he passed on at the ripe old age of ninety three. I suppose it`s some peculiar quirk of mine, but I hate funerals so much so, that I did not go to either of Mother or Dad`s funerals. Although I spent a lot of time away from home, that certainly didn`t mean that I loved Mum and Dad any the less. Quite the opposite in fact. My attitude is - show them you love them when they`re still here and able to appreciate it.

One other person whose visit to Alltyrodyn lingers in my memory was a girl called Serena, very top drawer, and coming from an excellent family, don`t you know. Much more to David`s taste in a social context. This in spite of the fact that she arrived with a rattle and a roar, mounted on an enormous motor bike, and clad from head to toe in black leather. At least she HAD been mounted on the bike. When she tried to pull up outside our front door, she must have hit a patch of loose gravel or something because the bike went from under her and she ended up flat on her backside, with the bike going full-bore several yards away. Full marks to the girl though, up she got, wrestled the bike onto its stand, switched off the engine and turned and greeted us most charmingly, all as if nothing had happened. Her clothing and transport perhaps make more sense when I mention that she was a lesbian. She didn`t make any sort of a pass at me, not that I`d have had the slightest interest if she had, but in any case we found out later that she was in a steady relationship with a French girl. Quite aside from this business of her sexual preferences, she was really excellent company and a good conversationalist on many topics.

In addition to the study of that blasted etiquette book, David himself did his best to tutor me in "The important social graces" and tried to ensure that I understood my place as the mistress of a large house. I learned the proper way to manage staff, how to act appropriately in any type of social situation, and how to be a good and successful hostess. I was still only about thirty years old at this time, and had learned many a lesson about life in the hard world of showbusiness, so there were many, many times when I blew my top at all this pretentious nonsense. I would then vigorously tell darling David in no uncertain terms just what he could do with Lady Trowbridge`s bloody book, Page by Page! I considered quite naturally I thought, that I was every bit as good as David`s parade of chinless wonders and snobbish airheads, and that if anybody didn`t like me as I was, then it was hard cheese for them.

Enough about people. Animals are superior to us in many ways I`m certain, and life in close proximity to them has its share of joys and sorrows. One thing is certain, you can never tell what is around the corner, let alone predicting what tomorrow will bring. Naturally, I had to pitch in with practically all the farming operations at least for the first couple of years when we couldn`t afford to employ farmhands on a regular basis. Two of the real "horror" jobs which I loathed were ear tagging the cattle and castrating the bull calves. It also used to upset me to go along to market and see the uncaring way in which many farmers virtually threw the calves into their lorries and carted them off to slaughter. During one particular fraught ear-tagging session, David and I were working our way slowly but fairly surely through the herd when we realised that we were right in the middle of a sort of rugby scrum, with large numbers of warm, pushy cows on every side. David was armed with the tagging machine, which looked a bit like a long, heavy pair of pliers, whilst I had the "easy" job of holding on to the cattle for the operation.

One of our prize Welsh Blacks decided that she wasn`t going to submit to the indignity of what we were going to do to her. Turning unexpectedly she lowered her head and pushed David backwards, eventually ending up with him being pinned quite firmly against the wall by her long sharp horns. Luckily the horns had only pierced David`s coat and not the man himself, but he looked very comical stuck there unable to move and totally helpless until she decided to withdraw. The things you see when there`s no camera handy! There`s a saying about the female being deadlier than the male, and that truism certainly applied to our herd of fine Welsh Black cattle. Our bull which we called Brenin (King), was a sweet and docile beast, completely unflappable, but his many wives were a different proposition altogether. Today of course, cattle are dehorned at a very early age as a matter of course, but during our farming days they were usually left alone, and many of them were equipped with quite fearsome weapons on the top of their heads. As the episode of David`s coat demonstrated, they knew how to use them too. This was especially true in early Spring when, after being cooped up indoors through the winter, they rejoiced in their freedom and frisked about all over the place. One special party piece was to charge at and thoroughly gore the mounds of dung which we`d placed ready for muck-spreading and to send it flying all over the place.

Although we later decided to concentrate on Welsh Blacks as giving a better return on our outlay, our very first purchase was a shorthorn cow. This senior animal, was christened by David, without any prompting from me I may add, and was known ever after as Selina, just like David`s first wife. Had her memory only been enshrined in the persona of one of our cattle, perhaps things might not have been too bad and I could have lived with it. To add insult to injury, though (and I`m sure most people will find this incredible) David insisted on hanging a large portrait of the real Selina - the Honourable one - in a quite prominent position in the hallway. But wait! The absolute last straw was that he actually expected me to accept personal responsibility for seeing that the portrait was kept clean and regularly dusted. Obviously I should have told him exactly where to go, but that was one occasion when I found myself completely lost for words. In addition to our cattle we also kept some sheep and at one point were having to look after a number of motherless lambs. I had to feed these from a bottle of course and was forever getting them mixed up, as they all looked alike to me. I was keen not to make the mistake of feeding some twice and leaving others unfed, so I hit on the idea of painting numbers 1 to 5 on their backs. I know it`s a mistake to have favourites, but I`m only human. My real favourite was No.1 who was undersized and had a number of nasty swellings on the side of its face. The poor thing never thrived and didn`t last long even with my constant care. The other four survived successfully. We sold two and kept the other pair. One of these was a black faced ram lamb, whom we christened Larry. He was very affectionate and followed me around, rubbing his head against my neck whenever he could. The other lamb, Lawrie was speckle faced and more independent but he followed me around as well. Eventually however, Lawrie became particularly over bold, really blotting his copy book on one memorable occasion. I`d taken Richard, who was then about seven years old into the walled kitchen garden, and the lambs had followed us. We usually used to let them in there to graze anyway. Pete, our boxer dog was with us. Without warning Lawrie turned on Richard, obviously intent on butting him. Seeing the danger, I grabbed Lawrie`s horns and tried to throw him, just like cowboys do with steers at rodeos! I couldn`t get him over, and the result was that he turned on me. At this point, Pete decided to come to the rescue and went directly for Lawrie. The lamb, seemingly unafraid, lowered his head and gored Pete in the mouth.

The poor dog ended up with a torn tongue, giving him trouble with soreness of the mouth for a couple of weeks afterwards. I got some sort of control over Lawrie eventually and shouted to Richard to take Pete out of the garden. I managed to drag Lawrie to the gate, where I nipped out quickly and shut him in. This episode prompted our decision to sell both lambs to a neighbouring farmer, where they very soon settled in quite happily with his flock. Some weeks after selling the lambs, David and I rode over to see how they were getting on. David rode his black mare, while I was mounted on a roan gelding called Zipper. What`s in a name? We soon found out! Zipper without any warning broke wind, or in good Anglo-Saxon, farted explosively and in great volume. So much so in fact, that the stupid animal actually frightened himself, and bolted away with me hanging on for dear life. At last, I felt the saddle begin to slip, and prepared to meet my end. I slid round, still hanging on for dear life until I found myself underneath Zipper, looking up into his face. This must have had a calming influence, because he calmed down and stopped, all as if nothing had happened. I replaced the saddle, mounted and rode back with my fingers firmly crossed.

It was impossible for me to carry out all the housekeeping duties and work on the farm, so it wasn`t too long before we began to look for some help around the house. I had mixed feelings about this as I wasn`t too happy about the prospect of ordering other people about, but it was obviously in keeping with David`s perception of himself as the squire surrounded by servants. The local folk showed quite a bit of interest in the idea of working at the big house, something which surprised me a little. Nevertheless active interest there was, and we began to recruit staff. The first of these was a young girl of about eighteen named Gillian, who took to the habit of addressing us as "Master", "Ma`am" and "Master Richard," like a duck to water. In no time she became the perfect little servant girl, always willing to help and with an almost permanent smile and air of happiness. It was quite a tonic to have her around the place. A little later on we also recruited an older lady, who had already seen some service in the house under its previous owners, and was very much of The Old School. She took Gillian under her wing and certainly did a lot to complete the youngster`s education. As a result Gillian became quite indispensable, a real household treasure, in spite of her youth. Her laundry was impeccable, to the extent that I`ll admit that it was she who taught me the very best way of ironing shirts and blouses and how to fold them beautifully. Another admission I have to make is that my standards have slipped back quite badly since those days! Nobody in this world is truly perfect, and Gillian was no exception. Her preferred leisure activities left quite a bit to be desired, to say the least. Her boyfriend had a motorcycle combination, which he used for racing and bike trials. It was quite a sight to see them at weekends careering madly around corners with our little household treasure hanging precariously out of the sidecar.

Another former servant whom we engaged as our parlour maid was a tall, thin dour person who seemed very distant. It was a bit difficult to communicate properly with her on occasions, but we persevered and it was just as well that we did. She turned out to be another treasure about the house with her own high standards and honest to the core. No longer in the first flush of youth, she paced about deliberately rather than on winged feet and one of her favourite expressions was "Sorry Ma`am, I`ve gorn slow." In fact, there was rarely if ever any real evidence of her "going slow", or swinging the lead, and she certainly never earned anything in the way of a rebuke or reprimand. I slipped up quite badly in my dealings with her on one occasion, though, when I asked her "Miss Wright, would you take out all the silver and clean it please?" She answered "Yes, Ma`am and I am known as Wright." That really put me in my place. An illustration that servants of the old school like her, practised their own kind of snobbery, with clear-cut divisions between the various classes of servant. It was one way of ensuring that everything was `just so`, both above and below stairs. Even after this lesson I`m certain that I must have slipped up on other occasions as well, although I can`t remember the details. Perhaps I wasn`t cut out to be the grand lady of the manor after all. Another senior member of the serving staff was our housekeeper, who came in daily from her home in the nearby village. She was a very kind, homely sort of person just a bit old fashioned in her habits and outlook and wearing her long hair in the sort of bun which had been fashionable in the twenties. Her colourful flowered pinnies were invariably spotless, whatever she happened to be doing at the time. She was another of the old school and although she helped me practically in ever so many ways, she wasn`t backward in telling me off if ever I did anything which she considered wasn`t in keeping with my position. I sometimes wondered after one of her little homilies, whether I might have been a tramp or something in a previous existence! Her fund of knowledge was vast, and she advised me, carefully, and in the greatest detail how to manage the house efficiently, how best to control staff and how to motivate them - every mortal thing I could ever possibly wish or need to know. Like many country girls of her generation, she`d never had a lot of formal education, but made up for it with a tremendous wealth of good old common sense. I valued her help and advice and lost no time in putting it into practice to everybody`s benefit. On a number of occasions I would give her a small gift, which she would always receive with a polite "Thank You." Invariably followed by her own little catch phrase, "It will come in very`andy." She formed part of a sort of double act, in that her husband was also always prepared to help out, although his services were confined to farm work, at which he was both keen and conscientious. One unusual feature about him was that he was in fact a Devonian, who had learned to speak Welsh fluently.

Not surprisingly perhaps, David loved the role of host, especially when the guests were what he regarded as "suitable." He would throw parties at the flimsiest excuse, often at such short notice that the staff and I would find it almost impossible to cope. We also loaned out the house for such local and charitable events as the Hunt Ball, and for other fundraising functions. During the summer one regular highlight was that we housed the local otter hounds, together with the hunt servant who looked after the pack and various huntsmen and women. They took full advantage of the first class stabling and facilities for housing and feeding animals - human, canine and equine and also of our extensive grounds where hounds and horses could be exercised. We were entertaining guests on one summer evening and had opened the windows of the room to let in some fresh air. This was a mistake, because a number of uninvited visitors made use of these entrances without warning. We found ourselves entertaining, if that`s the right word, a fair number of pipistrelle bats. These are the smallest of our native bats, with bodies about the same size as a field mouse and a wingspan of about six to seven inches. Of course they are completely harmless to humans, but one of our female guests immediately had hysterics and dived behind the sofa. We were unable to persuade her that the tiny pretty little creatures hadn`t come to entangle in her hair or suck her blood. We went to get hold of some nets to try and catch them. No luck, their radar was far superior to our efforts and we had to wait until they themselves decided it was time to go.

At about this time we had acquired, or rather, had foisted upon us a large and boisterous boxer dog named Pete. He was the one who accompanied me outside in the middle of the night during the haunting episode. Our acceptance of Pete was in the nature of a sort of reprieve or stay of execution for him because he had already seen off quite a fair number of the village dogs and earned himself a death sentence. Some of his victims had been dearly loved, others were valuable animals. It didn`t matter too much to Pete. Somebody, we never found out who, had heard that David and I were animal lovers and we were a reasonable distance from the village, so it was decided to give Pete another chance and unload him onto us. There might have been some justification for this opinion because at that particular period we possessed, or perhaps were possessed by, pea fowl; guinea fowl; chickens; horses; our herd of cattle; a ferret and a variety of pet birds. Although just a tiny bit apprehensive about Pete, because his fame, or rather his notoriety, had preceded his arrival we agreed that he might be worth one last chance and took him in. He settled down immediately adopting me as his special pal and taking over as a sort of guardian for me. Although quite a mature dog he often behaved a bit like a puppy and showed no trace of his evil past. If ever I had to go away and leave him, he would pine, sulk and make everything and everybody around him thoroughly sad and miserable. As I mentioned before we had two quite separate staircases. Many was the time when I would be making my way up the main stairs to be met half way by Pete who would have galloped up the other flight and along the link corridor to head me off. This was a show of affection, and it was for some time a source of mystery to me as to how Pete had been branded as such a murderous beast. He showed impeccable manners towards all his fellow guests, whether they were furred or feathered and treated our human visitors of all ages wonderfully well. We found out in the end that the trigger for Pete`s descent into the role of assassin was the presence of OTHER DOGS! When any other canines were anywhere about the house or grounds, we made certain that Pete was kept securely confined, and we were able to breathe easy for the duration, provided this precaution remained in force. Once and only once thankfully, we found out what we could expect if ever there was a breakdown in security. Of all the times to happen, it occurred when we had the entire pack of otter hounds staying with us. Frantic searching of the house revealed no Pete. We ran him to earth in the field in front of the house, standing in the centre of a circle of hounds, all with their noses pointing inwards and not a single tail wagging. They were obviously about to jump in and tear Pete to shreds. For his part, he was sizing them up and trying to decide which one to tackle first. I was totally at a loss about how to deal with this, and so for once was David. The situation was beautifully defused by the Hunt Servant, who coolly walked over and called the hounds off. Fortunately or perhaps amazingly they obeyed him instantly, the circle broke up and a potential bloodbath was avoided. We dived at Pete and held him securely whilst the pack made its way back to the kennels. No harm done, but definitely once bitten, twice shy (no pun intended) honestly. We made sure that Pete was securely under lock and key on every such occasion from then on. Pete went courting we think, arrived back home a couple of days later with what appeared to be a chest disorder. We were unable to save him and he died of pneumonia. How I missed that darling dog.

Another memorable canine companion of ours was Joss, a black labrador. We bought him for the grand sum of two pounds fifty from the local dogs' home and we were rather surprised when they told us that Joss had full papers, meaning that he was registered with the Kennel Club as having full pedigree. In our opinion he had more than a dash of bull terrier about him and was far more powerful than the average labrador. Another surprise was that one of the kennel maids came over just as we were leaving and sprayed Joss liberally with a powerful deodorant all over his rear end. As far as we knew, this type of thing was only done to bitches to disguise the fact that they were in heat, and we couldn`t see the logic in doing this to a male dog. We soon found out what this was all about. Joss suffered from a severe wind problem, blasting forth from his rear end at frequent intervals. Probably as a result of this he had a sort of unpleasant ambience which followed him everywhere. Aside from this, our old Joss was a truly loveable creature, gentle and caring with all the other animals and birds, and wonderful with children. Unfortunately this made him less than ideal as a guard dog. If anyone broke in to steal, he might well end up helping them along! For a short while we cared for a small terrier pup while its owners were away. It used to get into the basket with Joss and generally play hell nipping and pulling his ears quite unmercifully. Joss didn`t mind a bit and they eventually settled down to sleep together. Joss developed a hormone deficiency which degenerated into a form of alopecia. This meant that he lost practically all his hair except for some isolated areas on his head and paws. As may be imagined, this made him very unsightly and was obviously a distressing condition. The vet put him on hormone replacement tablets without any success and couldn`t really offer much comfort in the long term, either. In fact we discovered eventually Joss was undergoing a sex change. Dogs used to follow him around in the fond belief that he was a bitch in heat. When they found out the truth however, they would generally go for him quite nastily and many times he became the victim of bites. A neighbour had to dive in to rescue poor Joss on one occasion only intervening in the nick of time to prevent a fatality. His docility tended to work against him, and he would put up with quite a lot of aggression before retaliating. Eventually he lost the use of his hind legs and we very regretfully agreed that he would have to be put to sleep.

I could never come to terms with the hunting and killing of otters. They are such lovely and delightful creatures. The mores of the time dictated that otters were a scourge of the angling community. We were estate owners of about half a mile of fishing rights on the River Clettwr, which meandered through our fields. This formed a significant part of the estate boundary. It was an excellent salmon, trout and sewin river, attracting keen not to say affluent fishermen from all over the place. As owners of this valuable resource we owed a duty of care to preserve stocks, and this could best be done by exterminating "those damned fish thieves." Present day conservationists have taken my side and are trying to see that the otter population is protected. Not so during the fifties. David loved the whole idea of the hunt. It was central to his role as country gentleman and I kept my views to myself for a long time, because I was only too well aware of the reaction I`d have received if I`d tried to push my own opinions at him. It just wasn`t worth the row.

Although he was happy to kill, and to encourage the killing of certain species, David was otherwise extremely kind and caring towards other types of birds and animals. David would take in injured birds and beasts, whether we`d found them ourselves or they had been brought in by neighbours. He was perfectly happy to lavish kindness and attention on these poor creatures without stint, very frequently succeeding in restoring them to full health. He`d never had any kind of veterinary training to help him understand what he was doing, but then, love is a very powerful force and it can sometimes work what seems like miracles. In the years before we met, David had kept, trained and hunted with falcons, studying the subject in great detail and acquiring enough information to enable him to write an authoritative book on all aspects of falconry. I`m sure I could have found this quite interesting and even a little less disturbing than many other forms of hunting, but David seemed to have lost interest in the subject, and never attempted to start it off again during our time together.

Another of David`s quirks as the squire and country gent was his ridiculous insistence that we should dress for dinner, even when it was just the two of us. With hindsight, there might have been a modicum of sense in our changing out of smelly farmworking clothes and at least pretend we were gentry. In actual fact, it must be admitted that our dinner clothes consisted of my one and only long formal black dress, whilst David`s dinner jacket was at least thirty years old and quite literally green with age. He was far too mean to consider re-equipping either of us with more up to date outfits. Whilst on the subject of wardrobes it might be mentioned that practically all David`s gear was of about the same vintage. He dismissed any criticism of this by insisting that his clothes were made by THE best tailor in London. A chap called Anderson. I`d never heard of him and I never met anyone else who had, but that was David`s reason, or excuse and nothing would make him budge from it. He wouldn`t consider placing his tailoring into the hands of any provincial hobbledehoy, so the green dinner jacket and its companions soldiered on and on.

We carried on in this totally farcical manner for some considerable time, until the worm turned. I refused to put on what was left of my dinner gown, which had worn away in many places. In fact it resembled my costume at the Windmill many years before in that quite a lot of Simone was visible where it shouldn`t have been. Instead I came down to dinner in my dungarees. I really was having no more of this nonsense, nor would I pander to his pretensions any more. It was ludicrous, old hat and thoroughly unfashionable to dress for dinner, except on proper, formal occasions, I told him when we were dining alone. It bordered on the insane! There`s a saying about opposites attracting each other, but there`s also another one about birds of a feather. In David`s case, the latter was much more true. To fit in neatly with his eccentric family many of his friends were a bit dippy, to say the least, although this didn`t seem to affect their social acceptability. The business of dressing for dinner brings back memories of one of them in particular. This chap came down to dine in an exquisite and very expensive Hunt jacket in royal blue cloth complete with red lapels and all the trimmings and a pair of FLANNEL TROUSERS! He did have the grace to apologise, offering the excuse that he`d forgotten to pack his dinner suit trousers. "But it doesn`t really matter at all. Nobody will be looking under the table to see what I`m wearing." The same chap who came to our house on a number of occasions always got up and walked out immediately I sat down at the piano to entertain our guests. For a long time I thought he was trying to drop a hint about my pianistic abilities, but I later found out the truth. He was totally unmusical and only really appreciated the note of the hunting horn.

Although we were, by dint of hard work and burning a lot of midnight oil, starting to turn the corner financially, we still had constant rows about all manner of other subjects apart from money, coupled with David`s miserliness, I never saw the logic of always submitting to the will and accepting the opinions of my Lord and Master, so I`d kick over the traces quite regularly, frequently giving as good as I got. One fuse which got lit regularly was over Richard`s education. I would have been happy to have had Richard staying at home with us and attending the village school in Capel Dewi, quite close to Alltyrodyn. Although it was small, it was friendly and efficient, he was well settled there and quite happy. As a sort of bonus,

Richard`s Welsh was coming along very nicely as a result of going there. He complained on occasion that David and he spoke very different Welsh and "Daddy doesn`t understand me." I found out that Welsh varies in its vocabulary much more than English. There are greater contrasts in Welsh than even the difference between Devonian and Geordie English. Perhaps an illustration is called for. Take the simple sentence "The boy and the girl went to fetch the milk." In South and most parts of West Wales this would be rendered as "Fe aeth y bachgen a`r ferch i ol y llaeth." In North Wales however, the very same sentence would read "Fe aeth yr hogyn a`r eneth i mofyn y llefrith." Even non-Welsh speakers will appreciate the problems this sort of thing can cause.

Just after Richard`s seventh birthday, David came out with what can only be described as an ultimatum. No matter what, his son was going to have the benefits of "A High Class Education," and this would start forthwith. He was to be moved to a residential prep school near Aberystwyth. In spite of being out in the country and far away from city fogs and pollution, Richard was still dogged with asthma, and his muscle tone hadn`t really improved all that much, so both he and I were very unhappy at the prospect of his being moved from under my eye as it were. I suggested as a possible alternative that perhaps he`d be better off if he attended a special school which was only about five miles away and which catered very well for children with all sorts of health problems. It enjoyed an excellent reputation. As a result of his continued ill health throughout infancy and early childhood, Richard had missed quite a lot of schooling. The inevitable result of this was that he was rather badly adrift with some of his lessons. I thought that the atmosphere at the special school would be more encouraging and helpful, having had experience of handling similar cases over the years and that attendance there would be of more benefit to our son.

No good of course, David`s mind had been made up, so off we went to register Richard at Abermad school. Many tears were shed by both of us but to no avail. At the beginning of term, away went Richard to start his "superior" schooling. To be fair to all concerned Richard`s deep unhappiness and his health problems were seen by the staff at Abermad almost as soon as he arrived there, and the Matron actually told us that it would be best for everybody concerned if he were to transfer to the sort of special school which was set up to cater for children like him. For a few seconds I thought, "Exactly what I`ve been trying to tell David all along. Now he`s heard it from a professional, perhaps he will take notice." As far as David was concerned the good lady might just as well have saved her breath. A rather sad and apprehensive little boy was therefore left in the clutches of the public school system, and I just had to cross my fingers and hope for the best. When it became apparent that David was going to have his own way come what may, everyone seemed to be quite happy to rally round and do the best they could for Richard. Obviously he did derive some benefit from the small class sizes enjoyed within the public school system and the school`s sports master went out of his way to help Richard with special strengthening exercises. This regime did help Richard to make some reasonable progress, but I`m quite sure he would have been better off at the special school and under my own care at home.

Richard boarded at Abermad during the week and over most weekends as well, but he and many of the other boarders did come home, although fairly infrequently, on a Friday night, returning to school on the Sunday in time for supper. There was a fairly reasonable train service from a nearby station at that particular time so the journey even on a Sunday posed few problems, although it was one which dear old Dr. Beeching later closed down. As we prepared to leave after one of these weekend visits, I was rather surprised to see Richard sitting on his luggage trunk in the hallway, with his hands together and his eyes shut tight. "What are you doing Darling?" I asked. "I`m praying that I`ll miss the train and won`t have to go back to school," he answered. I shared his feelings on that subject but I dared not let him see that, so I put on my best face and off we went. Although we set out in plenty of time as usual and weren`t delayed in any way, we got to the station just in time to see the train disappearing into the distance. It`s things like that which make one wonder about the power of prayer and so forth. On another Sunday we were saved the train journey by some friends who called and offered Richard and me a lift to school. Their son also attended Abermad as a weekly boarder, so we accepted the offer gladly. Amazing as it may seem, we still had the 1925 Talbot, but it was going through one of its unreliable phases and Mid/West Wales on a Sunday is one place where one should not break down. We piled into their car and off we went.

Our route lay through the market town of Lampeter. A little bit like a cemetery on a Sunday with only the birds, beasts and chapelgoers showing signs of there being any life in the place at all. As we passed the shops, I noticed that one of them had a sale, which was due to start on the following day. Right in the centre of the window reposed THE most wonderful hat. We stopped, went back to the shop and stared. I decided there and then that the hat was going to be mine, come what may. My friend agreed that it would be a good buy and it would suit me beautifully. All the way to Aberystwyth and back I was scheming and plotting how I was going to get to Lampeter next day in time to beat all the other shoppers and grab MY HAT. Public transport there was none, buses only ran through our village on market days and they were few and far between, and the ancient Talbot was out of the question, being more rusty than trusty just then. Needs must however, so I commandeered the only vehicle available. Ye olde Fergie tractor, good for about 15 mph, with a following wind. I set off at the crack of dawn next morning. The only suitable clothing for driving the tractor was my far from natty farming gear. Dungarees and wellies, but what the heck, my money was as good as anybody else`s and they`d just have to take me as they found me. Off I went to drive the nine miles to Lampeter. My plans worked, and I pulled up outside the shop just as they were opening, parked the tractor and strode into the rather swish premises. I tried the hat on, although it didn`t really complement the rest of my outfit, decided that I`d been right all along and bought it. The staff couldn`t do enough for me, complimenting me on my choice and completing the affair in record time, even with the hat on. I certainly didn`t do much for their image! I placed the hat carefully in the rusty link box behind the driving seat, where it sat snug and proud, as I banged and smoked my way home. David thought I was quite insane but even he had to admit that it was a smashing hat and that I`d done the right thing in buying it.

It wasn`t just Richard who suffered the odd health problem. I was visiting a neighbour one day when I was suddenly gripped by severe pains in my abdomen. Thinking these might possibly be hunger pangs, my neighbour offered me some of her recently made rice pudding. I ate quite a bit, it was delicious, but the pains became worse. The doctor was called and I ended up being whisked off to hospital with suspected appendicitis. Of course my system was full up with rice pudding, so I had to face the dreaded stomach pump, or they couldn`t have given me any anaesthetic. The sister in charge was kindness itself and I`m certain I couldn`t have swallowed that horrible tube if it hadn`t been for her encouragement. I was caught just in time it seems and made a full recovery. The poor woman in the bed opposite who had the same problem wasn`t as lucky as I was, she died the same night.

Nothing in life is totally good or totally bad and there were some benefits to be gained from Richard`s absence from home. I didn`t have to trek to and from the village school for a start, and for another thing, it fuelled my determination to get back on the stage, by hook or by crook, as my interest in things theatrical hadn`t dimmed in the slightest. I started by looking around the immediate area of our home and found there were all sorts of societies actively engaged in putting on shows of many kinds. Some of them were quite good and the members terrifically keen. So Wales or at least a little corner of it WAS the Land of Song after all! As might have been expected, David was totally opposed to the idea. "No wife of mine is going to get mixed up in that sort of activity," and so on. He conveniently forgot, and got annoyed when I reminded him, that had it not been for my stage career and his interest in nude ladies etc., he and I would not have met in the first place. I couldn`t come to terms with this narrow minded and hypocritical attitude of his, so the whole question provided material for a series of ding-dong rows between us.

Salvation came from a totally unexpected quarter. Throughout all the intervening years, I had kept up my friendship with Pat. The original one I`d first met at primary school. She was a fairly frequent visitor and a most welcome one, especially as far as I was concerned. Over a period of time and working on him visit after visit, she at length managed to persuade David that allowing me to pursue my thespian ambitions would be a very good thing, pointing out subtly that to deny me the chance to get on with something I knew, loved, and was good at, would be the ultimate in cruelty. Pat was a past master (or a past mistress I suppose), in winding men around her little finger and David eventually agreed to her proposition. Just to be certain Pat actually drew up a contract or agreement and got David to sign it! The paper stated that he had no objection to my seeking to return to the stage and would not stand in my way. Even then we hadn`t reached the end of the saga. David and Pat argued about the necessity for me to have appropriate and respectable clothes. David wouldn`t or couldn`t agree to see our point of view on this topic, so Pat took me in hand and we paid a visit to Derry and Toms in London, where she rigged me out buying my one and only dinner gown. It really was a good "posh frock" and I felt a million dollars every time I wore it.

There`s a sad little postscript to this tale of Pat. I received word that she had suffered a quite severe stroke, which left her partly paralysed, unable to speak, or to comprehend effectively. A terrible, terrible thing to happen, especially to her. She`d been such a happy vivacious person, always ready to help others. All her capabilities and intelligence come to nought as simply and unexpectedly as if she`d been struck by lightning, and with results which were just as devastating.

CHAPTER EIGHTEEN

Return To The Theatre

The first theatrical group I sought to join was based locally, not too ambitious and putting on the sorts of shows that were well within my capabilities, even after so many years of going rusty! I determined that this was going to be my salvation - let`s get going and enjoy it. I was happy to talk about this project with several of my neighbours and friends, who all wished me luck in their various ways. One of them a farmer named Austin was always very friendly and helpful, in a purely platonic way I hasten to add. This in spite of the fact that David had once shot several of Austin`s sheep for "trespassing on our land." Austin had a fine tenor voice and very soon became an indispensable member of our little company. He would burst into song at the flimsiest excuse, often singing all the way to rehearsals and back again. He had a very wide repertoire of ballad and airs mostly in Welsh and I loved to listen to them, over and over again. Probably because of my background as a professional performer, I was frequently picked for principal parts in the shows we produced, which covered a wide spectrum of musical theatre, and our efforts delighted audiences wherever we went. It wasn`t all down to me, however, because apart from myself the company already had another experienced and capable leading lady with terrific presence and a truly wonderful voice. She happily took on many of the specially difficult roles, performing them wonderfully well. During my time with the opera group, we threw quite a number of parties for them at Alltyrodyn. David met the other leading lady on several occasions. Just like members of most of our audiences, he was totally captivated by her, and actually told me that he thought he was in love with her!! By that time I was past caring what David thought or what he wanted, and it wouldn`t have upset me too much had he pursued an affair with her. He actually asked me if I would mind if he did!! She however, showing a lot more sense than I had, told him in no uncertain terms what to do and where to go.

Not content with appearing in theatres in Carmarthen and Felinfach, we became more ambitious and actually entered the Waterford Festival in Ireland on a number of occasions. I was fortunate enough to win a total of five awards, some for acting and the others for singing. The prizes were won in the face of severe and very capable competition, and consisted of beautiful pieces of the world famous Waterford crystal. These pieces are still among my most treasured possessions.

Simone as Cilli in Goodnight Vienna, at Waterford

The Waterford Festival took place in the Theatre Royal, set right in the middle of the city, and a place full of history and legend. Like many other theatres, there was a stark contrast between the public areas and the back stage broom cupboards and hidden away in impossible recesses under the stage, whilst front of house was lavish and glowed with years of spit and polish. The main feature of the auditorium was a huge and truly magnificent crystal chandelier. It was a few feet in circumference, must have weighed at least a ton and was a wonder to all who saw it.

My world was now filled with magic once again. These trips to Waterford showed me the strength of the bonds of brotherhood which seems to be a feature of the Celtic races, and underlined the feeling that the Irish expression "cead mile failte" (a hundred thousand welcomes) was far more than just three words. My next visit to the emerald isle was undertaken under very different and far less carefree circumstances but a lot of water will have flowed under the bridge before we get to that part of our story. There seems to be no way at this point of avoiding the construction "meanwhile back at the Farm...." because a lot had been happening there, and some major decisions were made by David, not all of which were to our benefit. As far as the outside world was concerned, we appeared to be a happy sort of family unit, although our son was still absent, throwing parties and entertaining our guests as befitted our "status." The reality was nevertheless quite different.

We had decided or rather David had, to cut the losses we were sustaining and give up on milk production altogether. This decision was motivated by several factors, but mainly because our cowsheds and milking facilities were in serious need of repair and needed a fortune spent on them to bring them up to any sort of acceptable standard. As an interim measure David bought and installed a milk bale, a rather sophisticated bit of apparatus whose exact function is a bit difficult to explain in a few words. A cooler is normally attached to this so that the milk enters the bale at a reduced temperature, thereby helping its keeping qualities. We found out the hard way, that the setup couldn`t cope when the weather was really hot and many gallons of perfectly good milk found its way into the drains, because it would have gone off in the time between milking and collection by the bottlers.

After having thus bitten the bullet and decided to give up on milk, our finances actually started to improve again and it seemed we were going to do quite well after all. We were now concentrating on rearing single suckling calves produced by our Welsh Black cattle, our contribution to the beef market. If only we had left well alone we could probably have become really prosperous. David however, keen to follow up on another of his innumerable interests, wanted to try breeding horses. I`d given up on the whole idea of arguing with him by this time, so off we went and invested a frightening amount of hard-earned money in buying three brood mares. Although we had all the bits of paper showing faultless blood lines way back, this purchase was really our first step on a very slippery slope. The costs of keeping and housing the mares, and meeting the all too regular vets bills were bad enough, but the stud fees demanded for the attendance of any sort of reasonable stallion were outrageous. Frustratingly for us, we could see that the purchasers of our mares' progeny were also doing rather well out of the deal. We weren`t so lucky. Our money began to disappear at a terrifying rate. In addition to the mares we also kept three other horses for our own use, and regularly followed the Clettwr Hunt. This was a pack set up and maintained by a syndicate of local farmers and was reasonably successful. I was never enthusiastic about any aspect of the chase or the ethics and motivation which lay behind it. I just enjoyed the fresh air and exercise. Apart from chasing foxes, we still maintained our former position as hosts to the local otter hounds. We also followed them on occasion. Another kind of excursion about which I was never too happy.

CHAPTER NINETEEN

A New Career In The Beauty Business

Apart from my necessary duties at the farm and in the house, I was still actively involved with the local theatricals. This interest led me into another sort of venture which helped me in my efforts to retain a bit of independence. It came about because of the fact that part and parcel of stage work is make up. I had always had a particular interest in this aspect of stage work and was quite expert in the appropriate skills. This interest coupled with my expertise, led me into further adventures following a chance meeting with a South African lady who had set up home in the area. She was very much larger than life with a tremendous personality. She was the sort of person who can completely fill a room the moment they enter it. She was called Helen Leighton-Davies (a hyphenated half Davies just like me, but very much more prosperous!) Her skills lay more in the sphere of retail business, but our worlds overlapped because she was seeking to exploit what she saw as a niche market, especially badly served in our little corner of Wales.

Helena had spent many years in a globetrotting lifestyle and by now had become tired of it. She determined to put down some roots, and bought a property just outside the small market town of Llandysul not far from our own place. One of her first positive actions after getting settled was to take a long hard look at the local fashion scene. The results convinced her that the time was ripe for action. She was really going to make some waves and introduce the local ladies to the delights of spending lots of money on clothes and all the little accessories that go with them. With this objective firmly in view she jumped straight in at the deep end and opened three boutiques almost simultaneously. One of these was in Cardigan, another in Newcastle Emlyn and the third in the pretty seaside town of Aberaeron. The first two towns had markets and a selection of shops which attracted lots of people from a wide area, whilst Aberaeron, although fairly quiet and genteel, was pretty well patronised during the holiday season.

The stock-in trade of these boutiques was of a type and standard well beyond the previous experience of local folk. They would have seen similar goods only during trips to such centres as Swansea or Cardiff, if indeed they ever ventured that far. Helena sold clothes; jewellery; hats; handbags and gloves. They were all of couturier standard and commanded premium prices. She iced the cake by offering a super, superior and expensive hairdressing service. As far as my part in the scheme was concerned, Helena`s idea was that I should run the Newcastle Emlyn setup as a manageress and also introduce the idea of high-class make-up to customers. My responsibilities in this direction included selling the products, demonstrating their use and offering a range of cosmetic treatments for skin problems. This struck me as a really great idea as our family finances at this time were really suffering. The horse business was still in full swing. The only fly in the ointment was how David would react to the news of my wanting to take a position as a "shop assistant." I needn`t have worried. Helena`s personality and her obvious prosperity totally bowled him over. Her double-barrelled name was inevitably seen by him as an obvious sign of good breeding so he raised no objection. Off I went to take up this new challenge. With hindsight and now fully appreciative of Helena`s flair and business acumen, I`ve come to realise what a tremendous compliment she paid me by even considering me as a member of her team. By now, I`d passed my driving test and had acquired a reasonable Mini which enabled me to travel all over the place, and to commute to Newcastle Emlyn daily. I could also carry my stock-in-trade around to show customers. Helena`s choice of cosmetics underlined her determination to offer nothing but the very best. The first firm from whom she bought was Orlane of Paris, a very high class company owned by the Comte d`Orlane and his family and with branches in all the world`s capitals. Although enjoying a fantastic reputation throughout the continent and in the U.S.A., the firm was not at all well-known in Britain at that time. Even today the company`s name doesn`t feature in the top five or six cosmetic companies. Nothing daunted off I went to their London salon to begin my training in products, methods and techniques.

The training itself and all the other happenings and events which it entailed proved a most interesting and rewarding venture for me. Although I spent the majority of my time at the shop in Newcastle Emlyn, I was also involved in a whirligig of promotions, shows and so forth. These usually took place in the major stores which were being encouraged to stock the cosmetics. As well as the super shops in the provincial cities throughout the U.K., the company was able to gain a worthwhile footing in London where I worked on a number of occasions. I was involved, though quite a bit later on, in a couple of other promotions in Paris in Galleries Lafayette and Liberté. Although the quality of the products became more than evident as soon as they were demonstrated, the sad fact that the name Orlane was still largely unknown caused us some headaches on many occasions. The cosmetic market is very competitive and putting a newcomer into compete with the multinationals who had already had household names and wide acceptance was really hard work. Unlike practically all the other suppliers who plastered their wares and their image on T.V. night after night, Orlane Cosmetics never undertook this type of advertising themselves. Getting our message across involved our using really high-pressure sales techniques which I hated. Even then our sales figures were not too good.

As soon as she became aware of these problems, Helena took another look at the market and decided to switch to the rather better known but still very exclusive, Germaine Monteil range of products. Although still not among the leaders, these products were accepted much more readily by the buying public, so we were able to adopt a far more laid-back approach as far as selling techniques were concerned. Both Helena and I welcomed this less stressful regime.

As well as clothes, accessories, makeup and hairdressing the boutiques offered a general grooming service, through which we prepared ladies for those extra-special events like weddings, the Masonic Hall and similar local functions. This was quite successful and there was quite enough going on in the area to keep me pretty busy most of the time. As well as carrying out the sales and grooming functions I also went the rounds of local organisations like the Inner Wheel (Rotarians Wives), The W.I. and Soroptimists where I lectured on techniques and gave practical demonstrations. These were really enthralling for all concerned. I was able to build a wonderful rapport with my audiences and life was good once again. This was more like it! Just a tiny shade more ladylike and acceptable than shovelling manure on the farm.

Still keeping a watchful eye on sales and product acceptance, and after a lot of thought, Helena decided on yet another switch and approached the Elizabeth Arden company to ask if they`d be interested in supplying our little set-up. They agreed to start initial talks and sent one of their management people to come down and discuss matters in detail. The meeting went exceptionally well from everyone`s point of view. Mutual agreement was reached quite quickly and I was asked to come up to London for even more training. Naturally no-one needed to twist my arm about that!

I took up this latest challenge with great enthusiasm, and completed the course with flying colours. As a reward, the Elizabeth Arden people presented me with a lovely fitted case, containing the most wonderful demonstration kit you could imagine. As a fully-fledged beautician and consultant my evenings and weekends became much more crowded with engagements, and I addressed groups large and small all over the place. My audience was now made up of a higher proportion of younger ladies, many of them were actually seeking to embark on the same sort of career as I had, and to take up posts similar to mine. In fact, there were quite a few of these currently on offer with various firms.

A few years flew by with me keeping busy and interested, but still quite heavily involved with the boutique in Newcastle Emlyn, when a totally unexpected series of events conspired to burst my bubble once again. Helena had been married for many years and was by now a lady of mature age. Much to everyone`s amazement including her own and her husband`s, she became pregnant and produced a lovely baby daughter. Everyone was thrilled of course and Helena doted on her late in life little treasure. When the little girl was eight years old, Helena became seriously ill and before anyone realised what was happening she suddenly slipped away and died. With her passing, all the impetus seemed to disappear overnight, the businesses were wound up and were sold, and I lost quite a bit of my own motivation. Heigh Ho at least I had a job to return to even if it was only muck spreading etc. Even after this I still managed to retain some interest in the world of make-up and cosmetics, keeping it alive mainly via my continuing connection with the local theatricals and so forth. My expertise in the paint and powder department certainly hadn`t suffered mainly as a result of all the additional know-how I`d acquired.

It wasn`t too long before I was offered another chance. One of the chemists in Carmarthen had heard about my background and decided to employ me part time as a beautician, to see what effect it would have on his cosmetic sales. There`s a hefty mark-up on many of these products, so if he could increase his sales, it would be very profitable to everyone`s benefit. I took the job and worked away quite happily for some time. In spite of the fact that I was now really a shop assistant, and that I was no longer working for an upper class lady, David remained silent on the matter. He possibly realised that even the few pounds I was earning were making a useful contribution to our depleted kitty.

In the meantime as well, Richard had progressed through his prep school, until at the age of about thirteen he was entered for the Common Entrance Examination, which could have led to a place at Eton or several other public schools. His maths let him down very badly, so even David had to agree that enough was enough and that he`d be better off finishing his education nearer home. He went to the local comprehensive at Newcastle Emlyn, more or less just filling in time until he could leave at fifteen. After he left school, he was successful at landing a job at the newly opened cheese factory in Newcastle Emlyn. It wasn`t a particularly glorious job and he tended to smell a bit "ripe" when he came home after work. Nevertheless it enabled him to show a reasonable amount of status and self-respect and he was able to make some sort of meaningful contribution towards his bed and board.

Without any prior warning, David announced his intention of selling up lock, stock and barrel and moving to Ireland to set up a similar operation over there. I can`t see for the life of me what his motives were and he certainly didn`t explain. The next thing I knew was that we were tearing down the road to Fishguard to catch the ferry to Ireland in his recently acquired Austin Healey Sprite. This was a smaller economy version of the famous Austin Healey Roadster, with me hanging on for dear life. Some time previously he had actually managed to find a fellow Talbot enthusiast, (or maybe just an idiot) and sold the ancient 1925 car for a full hundred pounds. He then purchased this quite snazzy sports car, admitting he was partly motivated by the possibility that it would impress me! The "extra" in the form of high speed driving on David`s part was also put on for my benefit and was a bit of quite unnecessary macho bravado. He invariably left home in plenty of time for any appointment and this Fishguard trip was no exception. We stopped at an hotel for tea, but I was still shaken from the journey and couldn`t eat or drink a thing.

On the ferry, David was suddenly taken ill. The ship`s doctor was called, he examined David and declared that he`d suffered a slight heart attack. This was really nothing new. He was already on medication prescribed for a similar episode some time previously. Anyway after a couple of tablets and some rest, the doctor pronounced him fit and well enough to carry on, so we disembarked on Irish soil with David all set up and raring to go. In spite of having such strong feelings about the move to Ireland, he hadn`t done any sort of research or fact-finding at all. His attitude was "When I see the place I want, that will be it. We`ll sell up and restart over here." This trip was a repeat of our search all over Carmarthenshire before we found Alltyrodyn in fact, but the whole thing was compressed into a much shorter time scale. We travelled hundreds of miles all over the place, seeing all manner of holdings in every shape and size imaginable and fitting in visits to Cork and Blarney Castle. He insisted I should climb up and kiss the Blarney Stone, whilst he remained at ground level unable to manage the steps. I did as he wanted which seemed to please him. One or two of the estates we saw had made an impression on him, and he said that he`d have to spend some time thinking over the pros and cons of the matter before finally deciding which one of the properties he would buy. Nature was against him however, because he had another more serious heart attack soon after our return home and had to spend some time in hospital in Llanybyther. He suffered this attack while working on the farm. David was being helped by Gilbert, our Welsh-speaking Devonian and a young local lad called Delwyn, who was learning the ropes at the time, but later became quite expert. They found David lying under a tree, obviously very unwell and practically unconscious. Whilst at the hospital he very nearly died, He said later that he had had a near-death experience. He told us of the pleasant feeling that he was floating out of his body, all his pain having disappeared. Then he recalled hearing the nurses saying "Lift his legs," and he gradually recovered.

CHAPTER TWENTY

Separation

It seemed that David was totally unable to come to terms with the fact that he had a wife and son, who were human beings like himself and who also deserved some sort of life. Our quarrels intensified, both in frequency and in content, and he became so thoroughly obnoxious that we parted again, just like as we had in the Oxted episode. The trigger for this was the fact that I`d totally lost interest in the sexual side of our shell of a marriage. My relationship with David had reached the stage where it had become impossible for me to love him any more, indeed I didn`t even like him if it comes to that, and I preferred to sleep alone. He flew into one of his rages when I refused to give him his conjugal rights, and he practically threw Richard and me out of the house. This after having suffered a couple of heart attacks says a lot for his constitution I suppose. Frankly I was glad to go, because I didn`t feel I could trust him any more. He never actually hit me, or ever threatened to do so, but his tongue was an effective enough weapon and his verbal thrusts and barbs, against which I had little or no defence did a lot of damage to my self-esteem. Mental cruelty was not deemed sufficient grounds for divorce. Even then you had to prove adultery, and there was never any real question of David betraying me in that regard, in spite of the little matter of the operatic leading lady I mentioned earlier.

The pressing problem was one of accommodation. We`d been thrown out in the best tradition of Victorian melodrama, with basically the clothes we were wearing and little else. Luckily i was able to secure a roof over our heads at least in the very short term from one of my friends in the opera group. She was a real godsend taking some of the immediate pressure off me whilst I took stock. I had a good look around for something more permanent, but without success. In the meantime my friend had been canvassing several of her own contacts and managed to come up with a flat via an influential member of the local authority. Knowing I couldn`t be too choosy I grabbed the opportunity knowing that at least I had somewhere to live. I had to return to Alltyrodyn on a number of occasions to collect my own and Richard`s personal belongings. Many of my things were gifts from my Father, and were of sentimental value. There was also my small but important collection of Waterford glass. David, running true to form gave a perfect example of the dog in the manger refused to part with anything and created such a hellish scene that I ended up having to call the police. Peace of a sort was restored, but it was evident that my son and I stood little chance of effecting any sort of reconciliation, even if we had wanted to do so.

We gradually put the past behind us and were beginning to see some happiness together until I realised that I was being followed. Today`s expression is being stalked. David was still being the dog in the manger, and following me everywhere. Things really came to a head when I answered the door one evening and found myself looking down the barrel of a revolver. I knew David had kept his service revolver from the First World War, because he`d shown it to me on one occasion, but I`d certainly never imagined myself being on the sharp end of it! I slammed the door in his face and stood there shaking for what seemed like hours until I calmed down enough to phone the police and tell them all about it. Because they already knew about our marital rows they took my story seriously to the extent of offering me a certain amount of police protection. There was also the possible serious charge of possessing an unlicensed firearm to be taken into account. A thorough search of Alltyrodyn and the grounds failed to find either the weapon or any ammunition for it. David was friendly with a chap called Cayo Evans who was a leading light in the Free Wales Army which was making its presence felt at the time. Although they confined their activities mainly to painting over English signs and daubing slogans on walls and buildings, rumour told tales about arms training in isolated places and that these guerrillas were preparing for an insurrection. Be that as it may the whole thing fizzled out after a few years. I did wonder if David had dumped the gun with his friend.

Some time after the gun incident, Mrs. White, our housekeeper at Alltyrodyn, phoned to tell me that David had suffered another very serious heart attack. I`d given her my phone number just in case of any emergencies with a request not to divulge it to David. I couldn`t envisage any reason for David and me to telephone each other about anything in the normal course of events. We`d done all our arguing face to face over the years after all. When we got to the house he was sitting up in bed and surprisingly lucid and calm - not to say friendly. He advised me to give Richard something to eat saying "He looks as if he hasn`t had a square meal all day." He talked about the process of dying and recalled his own near death experience. Now that the chips were really down I must admit that I admired his bravery. He must have known that the end was very near for him. At the time and throughout all the years we were together, I never remember him showing an ounce of fear about anything.

This last heart attack was to be the last in the series which David suffered. Within hours he had passed away, quite peacefully and it was down to me as his next of kin to make the funeral arrangements. As holder of the King`s Commission twice, he was entitled to a full military funeral with all the trimmings, a right which he had made plain he intended to exercise when his time came. For some obscure reason which was never properly explained to me, the service was to be held in a small village some miles outside Wolverhampton of all places. I recall having a difficult journey following the hearse, which travelled at considerable speed. There was no M5 motorway in those days, and the route to the Midlands was a long drag across country and through town centres. I thought we`d never get there.

As I`ve already mentioned practically everyone within David`s family circle was to say the least just a little bit eccentric. This was underlined at David`s graveside of all places when his younger sister started making sheep`s eyes quite blatantly ogling the young bugler who was there to play the last post over the grave. Quite aside from any considerations of propriety she was old enough to be his grandmother, and just a touch unattractive. I was in two minds whether to be disgusted or amused by the whole episode. This silly little incident actually reminds me of another uncomfortable occasion when I was in the sisters company. They had come up to London where I happened to be at the time, probably on one or other of my training courses. I made the mistake of offering to show them the sights. Their clothes were a bit outlandish and would have been sniffed at even at a local jumble sale whilst their hairstyles and makeup were virtually indescribable. The younger sister (the bugle fancier), had long blonde hair hanging in rats tails, thickly applied dead white makeup and scarlet lipstick. Her elder sibling wasn`t much better either and it was amusing and amazing to see how heads turned to stare at them, even in the more outlandish parts of London, where abnormality is quite usual. Fortunately for me the two weirdos were accompanied by David`s nephew, Gordon, who was reasonably normal. He and I walked a few steps behind Les Girls, trying to look as if we didn`t belong to them at all. Gordon was the only son of David`s step brother Harold. Just like David, Harold it appears had a weakness for showgirls, and courted and married one of the famous Gaiety Girls. It might have been part of the reason for David`s personal spite and bitterness to learn that Gordon had made it to the dizzy heights earning a commission in His Majesty`s forces. This didn`t last too long however, as the poor chap died abroad whilst still only in his forties. Still he`d succeeded in becoming a Colonel. No mean feat at that age!

Colonel Gordon Lloyd-Davis (nephew)

For a short while I thought that David`s splenetic attitude and temper might possibly have died with him. Not a bit of it, as I found out at the will reading. His frustration at having a son who unlike his nephew was not cut out to be an Officer and a Gentleman was made all too plain, as was his desire for revenge on me. He had left instructions that all keys to Alltyrodyn were to be kept in the possession of Mrs. White and not handed over to me under any circumstances. Access to the house which had been my home for all those years was to be denied. Another great shock was in store, as we found out some time later, when David`s will was read. He left not one penny to Richard or to me. The entire estate was left to his two maiden sisters, who were even more eccentric than David had been. The sisters and I hardly knew each other. We hadn`t really spoken even at the funeral or during the London episode, and it was certain that David had made sure they had the lowest possible opinion of Richard and me.

As well as the unfairness of personal spite, the well-known Law of Natural Cussedness comes to the fore in this context. Had David lived just twelve months longer, my son and I would have had the protection of the Matrimonial Homes Act, and been assured of at least a fair share of the market value of the estate. All I was able to secure for us was an ex-gratia payment of twelve thousand pounds which wasn`t a fortune by any standards, considering the size of the estate. Nevertheless it was enough to help us in the purchase of a small cottage in the village of Nantgaredig, not too far from Carmarthen. David`s will included a good and productive agricultural estate of 475 acres, a farmhouse with outbuildings, a mansion house with a total of 18 acres of ornamental garden two cottages and a mile and a half of fishing rights on the River Clettwr. Even applying the values of about fifty years ago my legacy of twelve thousand begins to look a bit mean, especially when one remembers that quite aside from the building and land, there was also a fair bit of machinery and all the livestock to be taken into account.

CHAPTER TWENTY ONE

A New Life

By now, I was no longer in the first flush of youth, but a woman of forty plus. I`d always looked after myself physically and I hope mentally as well, and considered that I could still be thought of as attractive. On the minus side I`d been trapped in what was very obviously a loveless marriage for a huge slice of my life and I was all too aware that lightning can strike more than once. The possible trauma that would result from another wrong relationship made me very wary indeed, so I faced a quite serious dilemma. I can`t deny that I felt the need for some worthwhile male companionship but I was reluctant to commit myself, knowing of all the problems which could so easily arise. As I saw it, I was faced with three possibilities in my search for an unattached male of similar age. Firstly he could be a crusty bachelor set in his ways and impossible to live with in harmony. The second choice would be a widower, with the ever present possibility of his comparing one with the "dear departed" to one`s detriment, as a rule. Third and last would be a divorcee a little bit like buying a second hand car in some respects. Some are quite okay but in other cases you do get landed with someone else`s trouble. Perhaps I was being a bit too choosy myself - I don`t know, but I also had Richard to consider and his needs were important as well as my own. He`d grown up so far virtually without a father, or certainly without the affection and interest which a more normal father would have shown his only son.

In spite of all these problems and dwelling on the cons rather than the pros or maybe in a strange way because of them, I became attracted to Bill a fellow member of our opera and drama group. Obviously we had a lot in common and he was excellent company. Things progressed as they have a habit of doing sometimes until I found myself head over heels in love with the chap. My feelings were obviously reciprocated which meant that everything in the garden was lovely. I felt like a teenager again! His commitment to me went as far as leaving his wife and helping me in the purchase of the Nantgaredig cottage. Richard and I moved in with him and we lived there together for ten years. It was Bill`s influence which had enabled me to get hold of the flat in Carmarthen. Some time afterwards he admitted that as soon as he had met me it was love at first sight. He had been determined to do all he possibly could to help me out. After we had moved in with him we were perfectly happy and one of the real highlights was that we frequently went on the most fabulous holidays together, both at home and abroad. As far as the musical side of life was concerned we also made our mark on a number of occasions as a duo. Bill was an excellent pianist and in constant demand everywhere.

Although we were quite happy, after a little while I began to feel a bit guilty about the fact that I was not contributing financially to our household expenses. I decided that I would have to get some sort of a job and earn my keep. I succeeded in finding a job as a barmaid at the rather swish Ivy Bush Royal Hotel in Carmarthen, and I`m sure my application was accepted because I told them I`d enrolled on a Hotel Receptionists course at the nearby College of Further Education at Pibwrlwyd. Just to ice the cake as it were, I also took and passed O Levels in English Literature and French. The course content was extremely interesting and I`m quite certain that my experience of a good cross section of life helped me along with it. Hotel receptionists get to see and learn quite a lot about human nature after all! By now I was quite well into my fifties and therefore able to be a sort of mother or grandmother figure to the youngsters who were on the course with me. We were just like in the ATS, all girls together, following a common stream to a common end and we got on wonderfully well with each other. At the end of the course we all "Passed Out." Not in the unconscious sense of course, although end of term `booze ups` may have produced that effect, and went to work. Part of the course had involved our being seconded to hotels over quite a wide area, so that we could learn various aspects of the job in different surroundings. Some things came far easier than others. I found the operation of the Sweda accounting machine to be pure hell, and spent many hours wrestling with the damn thing. This meant that I got home late which didn`t help my stress level one bit.

At the time, in addition to having to earn a crust, I was coping with housework, three labradors and the needs of Bill and Richard. The situation was also just a bit complicated by the fact that Richard seemed to resent my having another man close to me, something he`d never had to experience with his own dearest Dad. Something had to give, so I decided I`d have to pack in the receptionist job and go back to part time work behind the bar. It didn`t pay too well, but the hours and conditions were a lot more civilised and enabled me to spend a bit more time with Richard among other things. We`d had to come to terms with the fact that Richard was never going to excel at anything academic. In David`s view this was because of the unsatisfactory genes he`d inherited from me of course and he was very disappointed when his own high-flown plans came to nought. On the positive side Richard actually had quite a lot going for him. He had an excellent sense of rhythm and good timing, being able to follow music accurately on the radio. I began to wonder whether, given a bit of quality training he could be turned into a useful percussionist. At the time the cost of lessons was prohibitive, so this idea had to be put on hold for a while.

In the meantime the home situation eased somewhat after Richard discovered the joys of driving. These days he was never happier than when behind the wheel of a van or small truck. He was careful and reliable, but although several of the local businesses were perfectly happy to employ him on a casual basis, there never seemed to be anything in the form of a permanent position on offer. However, there was enough work to keep him busy and it wasn`t too stressful. He was again able to assert a bit of independence and to contribute a fair share towards the household bills.

As far as the opera group was concerned I was still going strong, taking leading or prominent roles in most of our productions. We performed old favourites like The Mikado and Gipsy Princess and one or two more adventurous ones like Good Night Vienna and Man of La Mancha, where I played the part of the housekeeper.

I played the part of the wicked stepmother in Cinderella; the witch in Beauty and the Beast and The Merry Widow twice.

Simone as Grizzelda the witch

I also appeared in Dick Whittington. One specially memorable incident occurred on the last night of a run of White Horse Inn, where I played the part of Josepha the innkeeper. In the final scene, Josepha goes into a close embrace with Leopold, the waiter. The lacings of my bodice got entangled with the buttons on the front of his uniform, and the pair of us just had to stand there, stuck fast for what seemed like ages, until we were finally able to struggle free. That scene really brought the house down, but I`ve never had any hankerings to repeat it.

Encouraged by these successes, and having regained a lot of my former self confidence I began to consider whether there were some possible semi-pro openings in the local showbiz scene, so I teamed up with a girl called Eryl, and we went the rounds of local venues as a Country and Western duo. We continued like this quite well for a fair while, but then I noticed Eryl`s attitude changing. She became very attentive and "clingy" to quite an embarrassing extent, but I thought nothing much of it until the penny finally dropped. She was a lesbian and fancied me. Unfortunately for her perhaps, I have never had any leanings in that direction. I`d had quite enough problems with men, for heaven`s sake. The inevitable result was that our duo broke up in a series of rows which almost became a stand up fight between us.

Among my more recent stage and screen experiences whilst in the Carmarthen area were the infrequent occasions when I was able to land the odd bit part in some T V productions. Very little went on in that part of West Wales. TV was centralised in Cardiff, some 65 miles away. On the principle of having some extra irons in the fire, and thinking "nothing ventured, nothing gained" I dropped a line to BBC Wales. I was quite honest about my lack of actual TV experience and also about my inability to speak Welsh, but thought my wide-ranging background might just commend itself to some consideration. A pleasant surprise came with a return letter only a few days later, signed by John Hefin, one of the directors handling a broad spectrum of work for the station. He expressed interest in my application and promised that I`d be kept in mind if, and when, anything suitable came along. "Fair enough" I thought, "At least it`s a gentlemanly and polite put down." Luckily I was quite wrong. I very soon had an offer of a bit part in a scene depicting a protest march to try to save the Welsh Language. There was a terrific rumpus over this, because many of the onlookers were convinced that the march was a genuine one and several of them tried to join in.

Some time later I landed a small cameo part in a film about the Falklands campaign. I was seen at the quayside accompanied by a young woman with a baby. I was waving goodbye to my son, and she to her husband, who were sailing away on a troopship. The scene was terribly poignant so much so that the tears came freely and naturally. Even some of the technicians and crew were really affected as well. I ended up sobbing so much that John the director took me in his arms to let me cry on his shoulder. Although these parts were small and really unimportant, the fact that I was doing an acting job at all meant that I had to have an Equity card. I wrote to them with some misgivings as I had been out of the scene for nearly twenty years after all. Another pleasant surprise came with their reply. They said that there was no problem in renewing my membership, which they were happy to do. They welcomed me back on board and wished me luck and success for the future.

Within a couple of weeks after the Falklands film, I had a firm offer of quite a worthwhile part, which naturally I accepted immediately. I was to play the part of a tart and abortionist called Nans y Goetre. The production was called The Secret Room (Y Stafell Dirgel), a very meaty story involving rape, murder, religious intolerance and witchcraft set in seventeenth century Machynlleth. My part was quite minor really, with a small amount of dialogue, which was just as well as my Welsh was far from good. It included the carrying out of an abortion (simulated of course) on the leading lady. The heroine played by Liz Miles, actually dies as a result of my attentions, leaving her young husband grieving. All this takes place in just one episode!

Simone in The Secret Room

This operation was carried out in an ancient and very dilapidated cottage quite near Cardiff. At the time it was very nearly a ruin but has since been taken over, beautifully restored, and made into a cosy dwelling. The play had to show the filthy conditions that prevailed at that time, and the camera dwelt lovingly on the horrific array of instruments that were used. There was also a load of rubbish and some dead rabbits lying around. Before filming started, I had to go into the garden and dig my hands into the soil so that they were filthy, with my nails full up with dirt. For each take, I made my entrance by descending some old rickety stairs which were festooned with cobwebs. Talk about suffering for art`s sake! In another scene in the same play I appeared as the tart, trying to drum up business in the local tavern, flirting with every Tom, Dick and Harry and entertaining the audience by performing a traditional Welsh dance called Cadi Ha. It worked as I recall and I didn`t go home alone (in the play of course.) For these scenes make up department was told to highlight my boobs, although my costume was already very low cut. This struck me as over the top (no pun intended) because I`ve always been pretty well endowed in that region.

A little later on, I appeared in another costume drama called Off to Philadelphia in the Morning. This was set in 1850`s Merthyr Tydfil and was the story of the famous local composer Joseph Parry. David Lyn played Parry and Sian Phillips was the opera singer, Myfanwy. She was the inspiration for the world renowned love song which bears her name. I played the part of her devoted Cockney personal maid and dresser, for which I had to wear tight stays under my voluminous costume. Amazingly, I found the stays wonderfully comfortable, so much so that I ordered a garment for myself, to be made by a Swansea corsetiere. Unfortunately this was nowhere near as good as the original so it is still in its box at the bottom of my wardrobe. You just can`t win`em all can you?

The play was also memorable for the way it projected another member of the cast to the dizzy heights. She was a local lady called Donna, not much more than a teenager at the time, who played the part of the young Myfanwy. She was made up carefully to look like a real ugly duckling, and she was endowed with a real Welsh valleys accent you could cut with a knife! Donna had no real experience of theatre of TV. This was an unbelievably big break which came to her out of the blue. Luckily she was a real natural, who had enough good sense to grab the opportunity with both hands and really make something of it. Since Off to Philadelphia she has gone on to find fame and fortune in

Television, both over here and in Canada. Good for her I say!

It was about this time that I appeared in a role which should have qualified me for the Guinness Book of Records as probably the world`s oldest (or more mature) belly dancer. Actually I enjoyed the whole thing immensely and I couldn`t have been too bad at it, because I was invited to work at numerous clubs and also on board a cruise liner. In one variation to my technique I appeared on stage using a boa constrictor; a REAL one as a prop! The snake belonged to a fellow artiste who was quite a good friend. During my act the boa was draped around my forearm as I danced, and all went well until she really disgraced herself and did a whoopsy all over the stage. I beat a hasty retreat as can be imagined and never tempted providence again.

By now I had become really at home in TV productions and was beginning to enjoy the medium for its own sake. For the BBC2 production "Sea Tales" I beat several other hopefuls for the part of Ceridwen, wife of a philanderer who was carrying on with Jane Lapotaire. Jane was travelling by boat to her lover`s island retreat when I appeared to her out of the mist, in the form of a ghost or evil spirit, willing her to drown. As in all good stories my wicked wiles didn`t succeed and she finished the voyage safely ending up in bed with my hubby. This was another period drama, filmed in November just off the Pembrokeshire coast. Thank Goodness for eighteenth century costumes. It was bitterly cold, especially in a small boat at sea, and my dress served beautifully to hide the long johns and thermal vest I had to wear underneath. To add insult to injury filming went on for a very long time because the director and cameraman who were in a boat alongside us couldn`t agree about a single detail. They argued and tongue lashed each other incessantly while poor Jane and I sat there miserable and freezing. Still, we got it in the can eventually and the series proved very popular with viewers.

Some time after this I was literally thrust into the part of Mrs. Jenkins a cantankerous old biddy and mischief maker, in the first series of District Nurse. This was filmed in and around Tredegar and starred Nerys Hughes, a lovely lady whom I found most charming. The original intention was for me to appear as Mrs. Probert, a very small and unimportant role. The night before filming was due to start, the director phoned in a real tizzy. The actress booked as Mrs. Jenkins had been taken ill. Could I possibly take over? With a lot of trepidation I agreed to try. The script was sent round by courier arriving at 10.00 p.m., and I set to it to learn the part by the following morning. I set the alarm clock to ring every hour so that I could stay awake enough to have a go. It all came out right in the end. I learned the lines and delivered them correctly. Mary the director was over the moon and wrote me a very kind letter of appreciation, which has pride of place in my personal archives.

Turning up on site in Tredegar ready for filming gave me a tremendous feeling of deja-vu. By a strange coincidence one of my school friends many years ago had relatives in Tredegar and I accompanied her on quite a few holiday visits to the town. Tredegar was a typical valleys steel and mining town, and its claim to fame was that it was the birthplace of Aneurin Bevan, the founder of the National Health Service. In quite a few parts of the town, the houses still retained their original doors and windows so it was easy to find locations in keeping with the twenties setting for the series.

Another really lovely lady with whom I appeared more than once was Rachel Thomas who had earned the title of "The Original Welsh Mam." She was totally committed to her career and was a professional to her fingertips and a source of help and wisdom to all around her. I recall one of her tips: "Never go out in the cold without a hat. As you see I never do, and I`ve never had a cold in my life."

I had the delight and privilege of working with Ronnie Barker in his series about a Welsh photographer - "The Magnificent Evans." He made the whole thing look so easy; the mark of the true polished performer and never seemed to be down or miserable in any way. He kept us all amused on and off camera, and we often had to take scenes several times because Ronnie made us laugh so much and always in the wrong places. The other principal in the show was Sharon Morgan, with whom I`d worked in the Carmarthen amateur operatic society. She`d appeared with us as a dancer in White Horse Inn and her progress since was truly wonderful. In spite of success she was still the same unspoilt young lady she had always been. I played Bessie Williams in Dylan, Marjorie Long in Return of Truscott Reeve, and the Queen Mother in Woman He Loved. In the long running series Casualty I played the part of a Ward Sister.

Simone as a Ward Sister in Casualty

Moving over to Independent Television I secured a walk on part as a secretary in "Dinas", a rather upmarket local soap. This was probably too upmarket because it sank without trace after a couple of series. As far as I was concerned as well the part didn`t do too much to bring me to anyone`s attention, so I kept trying at the BBC. From them I was offered a regular walk-on part in "House of Elliot." This was filmed in London, which caused me a couple of problems. Still, you can`t make an omelette without cracking eggs, so I accepted the offer with good grace. In the first series I played a fashionable lady of no great account, although my dancing skills were exercised in a couple of ballroom scenes. In the second and third series, however, I got a more regular role, offered to me when the original actress had to go into hospital. I seemed fated to benefit from the misfortunes of others in this context! The part wasn`t quite so glamorous in this case. I was one of the dowdy workroom assistants downtrodden and unappreciated. I didn`t really mind this, because the money was quite good, and I was lucky enough to find a reasonable B&B only a couple of hundred yards from the studio. Depending on the shooting schedule, I would either stay overnight in London, or travel back to Wales between sessions. Generally speaking the hours spent on set were quite long, especially when changing and cleaning up time was taken into account; just like the Windmill in many ways. I often had to dash to catch the last train from Paddington at 11.30 p.m. This only went as far as Cardiff so I made arrangements to crash out overnight with a fellow artiste who lived near the city. I went home on a reasonably early train the following morning.

My swan song was my appearance in a cinema film. A remake of the classic "Suspicion" starring Cary Grant. Our version featured Anthony Andrews, and I played his housekeeper Mrs. Jensen. It was almost a `blink and you`ll miss me` sort of part, but I was still on set for quite a long time. Part of the action took place just outside Bristol and we were accommodated in a couple of really swish hotels in the city. I loathe the bowing and scraping which goes on in such places, so I asked if I could move somewhere simpler and cheaper - and they agreed! During the day on set I was allocated a quite large caravan, where I could relax between takes. I spent a whole day there on one occasion, because Anthony`s son was taking part in his school sports day. The company laid on a helicopter to fly Anthony to the school and back again so he didn`t miss out on his son`s sports. This was in spite of the film being described as a budget production. Needless to say he didn`t get back in time for any worthwhile filming to be done so the day was effectively wasted.

In the meantime my beloved sisters-in-law, heiresses of Alltyrodyn in which they took little or no interest, had grown older and (if that`s possible) more gag-ga than ever. By and by they went the way of all mortals and Richard and I were given another illustration of the depths to which my husband had sunk in his spite. Although I`d never expected anything substantial from the sisters, I did have a little hope that we might be granted a bit of the residual sums. Not a bit of it! We were told that David had made a proviso in his original will (that we weren`t told of at the time,) that nothing was to be left to his widow and son under any circumstances. The sisters' house was left to one of their neighbours who used to run errands for them and do a bit of housework, whilst the residue - a substantial sum was left to the Wolverhampton solicitor who had drawn up the will in the first place. This, I believe is the `ethics` of the legal profession. With a rather sinking feeling I took up arms and had a go at contesting the will. After quite a lot of to-ing and fro-ing, I managed to secure a small sum to cover the costs of some small items. These included bits of furniture and some small items which I had bought personally, and which therefore formed part of my personal contribution to the home. Perhaps this small sum was forced out of him by an attack of guilty conscience. I`ll never know the truth of the matter. It was then, and probably still is, a most difficult undertaking to try to engage one lawyer to sue another one. They are reluctant, understandably perhaps, to act against a fellow professional although win or lose they never seem to find themselves actually out of pocket. I must own up to harbouring a great deal of bitterness towards lawyers, but perhaps this is understandable, given the circumstances. I`ve always had a great reluctance to trust them to do anything for me, but I`ve had to go to law on a number of occasions since all this happened. We were grateful for the small sum we received and put the whole thing down to experience.

There was just one pleasant surprise to come as a result of the sisters passing. The second one`s death was reported in The Times, where it was seen by a distant relative of David`s. He phoned me out of the blue and introduced himself as Glynn, only son of David`s nephew Gordon. I`d heard about Glynn but he seemed to drop out of sight, remaining as a kind of long-lost relative for quite a few years. He subsequently came down to Wales to see me and meet Richard, and we all got on together very well. Just like his father, Glynn was a very nice chap, perfectly normal, well balanced and reasonable. I must have been extremely unlucky to have landed myself with the wrong branch of the family. Unfortunately we don`t know these things at the time, and thankfully I was well out of it by then anyway.

After Bill and I had happily shared the cottage for just over ten years, our little world broke apart quite abruptly. Bill received news that his wife was very ill. They`d never bothered about a divorce and he felt rightly or wrongly that his place was at her side. We talked the whole matter through and decided that it might be for the best if he did return home to help look after her, but Richard and I should retain our tenure of the cottage come what may. As an extra Bill also undertook to help us financially as neither Richard nor I was working regularly, and some of the household bills were more than we could manage. This arrangement continued for quite a long time. After we`d been apart for just over a year, Bill decided that it was high time that the garage adjoining the cottage should be dealt with. This was really not a moment too soon as the structure was a rickety corrugated iron affair, badly corroded and with innumerable holes in the roof. It was really well beyond repair and would definitely have to be replaced. In fact, I`m quite sure that the car got wetter after being garaged than if we`d left it in the open. Bill sought quotations from a number of firms and eventually fixed on one as offering the best value all round. The company sent their local representative to measure up and sort out the details. We got chatting over a coffee. His name was John, and he was a good talker and a listener and excellent company all round. He sussed out very quickly that I was alone and lonely and obviously took pity on me and my state of affairs. He told me, among other things that he wasn`t terribly happily married, and fully understood the problems of loneliness. He spent practically all his working time on his own, as his wife just wasn`t interested in travelling around with him. His territory covered some of the most beautiful countryside in West Wales, so that when he suggested that I might like to come along with him on his rounds I jumped at the chance. There followed as most people would have predicted, another falling in love scenario. This time it was all one-sided. John fell for me like a ton of bricks. He divorced his wife, to his obvious relief in the hope that we would now pair up, settle down together and live happily ever after. Unfortunately for his dreams of romance though, I could never bring myself to think of him anything more than a wonderful best friend. I was completely honest with John right from the start, and he seemed to accept the situation probably hoping that I would come round in the end. There`s an old saying that any iceberg will eventually thaw if the flame is hot and constant enough.

We sold the cottage soon afterwards and moved to Swansea where we lived in a reasonable terraced house with a marvellous view overlooking the sweep of Swansea Bay. This panorama could quite easily have made up for many deficiencies in the house, but it was in fact in a pretty good state of repair and quite comfortable.

By this time allowing for the sale of the cottage and the purchase of the Swansea house, I had managed to scrape together a total nest egg of about £4,500. or thereabouts, so I suggested that we capitalise on John`s knowledge of construction and go into some sort of partnership in the building, repair and development business. Although John had no real capital or savings he was keen and enthusiastic and took the idea on board immediately. It wasn`t long before we found a 300-year-old cottage in the village of Ystradgynlais in the valley of the river Tawe, some fifteen miles north of Swansea, which we bought outright for the bargain price of £2,500. Along with the property came a very welcome local authority grant, which helped us to turn the cottage into a reasonably up-to-date and cosy home. We pitched in together and I did what I could, but the vast bulk of the work was done by John. In order to save on travelling time and costs he moved in to a small caravan which we obtained and parked on a bit of waste land close to the cottage. At the time Richard and I stayed in the Swansea home.

Quite soon after we had completed work on the cottage, a prime plot of building land became available, also in the village and not very far away from the cottage site. Something told me to bid for the plot and to avoid offering a round figure. So I added an odd hundred pounds to my original estimate and my tender was successful. This I felt was the absolute right spot for our future home, quite close to the shops and amenities and with lovely friendly neighbours. Several people had already expressed an interest in buying the cottage, so we sold to the highest bidder and turned in a reasonable profit from our venture. It was this extra bit of capital which financed our buying the plot.

In the meantime in order to free a bit more capital, we sold the Swansea house and bought a medium sized bungalow right on the edge of the wonderful Gower peninsula. Richard and I moved in there while John started on the construction of the "home of our dreams," back in Ystradgynlais. Unfortunately it was at about this time that my TV career began to show signs of drying up and offers of parts came less and less frequently. The net result of this was that the construction of our bungalow took between three and a half and four years to complete. John lived there during all this time, never complaining and getting on with his tasks with a will.

In view of my past sad experiences with families, lawyers, wills etc., I thought it might be a good idea if I signed over ownership of the Gower bungalow directly to Richard. This was, as it turned out a very wise move on my part, but we weren`t to find that out until a bit later on. At this time Richard had landed himself a reasonably well-paid job with the Territorial Army. He got himself involved with all sorts of interesting jobs including playing percussion with the unit band. As I`d predicted some years earlier he was pretty good at this and soon earned a lot of respect for his ability. An added bonus was that every day brought something different. A fresh challenge to overcome. This was especially good for Richard as he could never have settled to anything boring, repetitive or humdrum.

This arrangement continued quite happily to the benefit of all parties until Fate stepped in again. John, who had always seemed so fit and well and active died very suddenly. With an awful sense of deja-vu I received phone calls and visits from John`s family just as loveable and sympathetic as David`s had been, all those long years ago. We`d never bothered to set out the terms of our partnership on paper, which was a big mistake. They demanded the `trifling` sum of forty thousand pounds being half of the value of the bungalow. Their grounds for this demand was that John had actually built the bungalow with his own hands receiving nothing in the way of payment from me. So I was left holding the baby again. Now I was faced with a pretty little dilemma. Should I move my own furniture out of the bungalow and sell it to see if I could buy the family off or stay, stick it out and see if I could raise a mortgage or some sort of loan to settle the matter. After a lot of anxious thought and not a few sleepless nights, I decided on the latter alternative. We were I suppose lucky in that we were able to use Richard`s bungalow as collateral, so the loan was arranged fairly easily. At the same time, it didn`t come cheap and monthly payments would be a burden for some years into the future. Galling to think that I`d be starting on a mortgage at an age when most people had paid theirs and could sit around with their feet up, free from care. In order to help with the mortgage payments, we decided to let the bungalow. This unfortunately turned out to be more of a headache than an actual help. We were very unlucky with our tenants and decided eventually to cut our losses and sell it.

I was still conscious of the need to keep myself interested and physically fit and as supple as my ageing joints and bones would allow. Naturally my mind is as sharp as ever, so I decided to do some voluntary work at a nursing home. My original idea was to help out as a nursing assistant, however after a while this aggravated my own aches and pains, so I reluctantly had to stop. I gritted my teeth at this setback and determined that I wasn`t going to give up on everything just like that. I wanted to carry on doing something for those stuck in the home. Many of them had fascinating stories to tell and we spent hours swapping tales of days gone by. We also hummed and sang lots of the old songs so I thought about putting on some community singing sessions. This proved a bright idea I`m glad to say. I teamed up with some other like-minded folk and put on shows for pensioner`s groups, hospital patients and all sorts, and our efforts went down really well.

I teamed up with a wonderful keyboard player, Gloria, when we toured OAP day centres, hospitals, nursing homes, in fact anywhere were entertainment was required. Gloria was a treasure,; she could transpose music to any key, and if any of the audience wanted to have a special song, she would be there. She had accompanied many well-known artistes. We had great rapport with audiences and even managed to get some of the audience to participate, even though they had been too reticent and shy. We had a great time!

Amal Dance

I also joined a belly dance group, there were about a dozen of us, all over the age of 60. I really enjoyed the sessions, and we took part in local variety shows. I loved the costumes with all the sequins and glitter and glamour. My fellow belly-dancers persuaded me to apply, and at the age of 84, I entered into the Britain`s Got Talent competition and actually got to the third round. The judges were: Piers Morgan, who was quite rude and said "I would not like my mother doing this at 84", he appealed to the audience and they shouted him down; Amanda Holden who was sweet and said "She is an encouragement for other old people to take up movement and exercise"; and Simon Cowell (bless him!) was also kind, he enjoyed my dance and said "I want to see this lady again." I found it an exciting exhilarating experience!

Now at the age of 95, I look back down the years, at all the memories of my life in showbusiness. I have loved every minute of it. I have shared my life with so many wonderful people, I have learned so much, for which I am so grateful and thankful.

Simone aged 95, 2017

24069424R00114

Printed in Poland
by Amazon Fulfillment
Poland Sp. z o.o., Wrocław